MODERN FUNK FUSION GUITAR

Seamlessly Combine Elements of Funk, Fusion & Blues Into Cutting Edge Guitar Solos

SHANE THERIOT

FUNDAMENTAL CHANGES

Modern Funk Fusion Guitar

Seamlessly Combine Elements of Funk, Fusion & Blues Into Cutting Edge Guitar Solos

ISBN: 978-1-78933-413-5

Published by **www.fundamental-changes.com**

Copyright © 2023 Shane Theriot

Edited by Tim Pettingale

The moral right of this author has been asserted.

All rights reserved. No part of this publication may be reproduced, stored in a retrieval system, or transmitted in any form or by any means, without the prior permission in writing from the publisher.

The publisher is not responsible for websites (or their content) that are not owned by the publisher.

www.fundamental-changes.com

For over 350 free guitar lessons with videos check out:

www.fundamental-changes.com

Join our free Facebook Community of Cool Musicians

www.facebook.com/groups/fundamentalguitar

Tag us for a share on Instagram: **FundamentalChanges**

Cover Image Copyright: Author photo, used by permission.

Contents

Introduction 5

Get the Audio 7

Warm-up Drills 9

Chapter One – "Big Timer" 13

Chapter Two – "Slow" 21

Chapter Three – "F Thing!" 36

Chapter Four – "Minor Bluesish" 42

Chapter Five – Minor Funk (Rhythm Part) 51

Chapter Six – Minor Funk Soloing Approach 59

Chapter Seven – Minor Funk – Advanced Soloing Ideas 69

Conclusion 79

Introduction

Most genres of modern music emerged from a melting pot of other styles. Soul, for instance, has its roots in R&B and gospel, while the origins of funk come from a mix of soul, R&B, gospel, and jazz. All types of music influence and inform each other, so whether you want to play modern blues, soul, or jazz, knowing how cross-pollinate their melodic ideas will greatly enhance your creativity.

Fusion is a term used to describe the blending of two or more styles into something fresh, and this book teaches you how to bring many exciting elements into your playing, underpinned by a healthy dose of funky soul grooves.

I grew up in Louisiana in a town not far from New Orleans. It's a state with rich and diverse musical influences, steeped in blues and jazz, Creole and Cajun music, and Afro-Caribbean rhythms. All these elements combine to create styles of music that are uniquely identifiable to the area. In this book we'll discuss how to approach different expressions of this music and look at a range of soloing concepts designed to give it a contemporary twist. Here's an overview of the soloing techniques you'll learn, all of which have become a part of my style over the years.

Modern blues

Modern blues players tend to have more tools at their disposal than the classic blues players who trailblazed the music and laid the foundation for us. This includes freshening up pentatonic soloing by breaking out of standard scale patterns, omitting notes to create more spacious-sounding intervallic lines, and superimposing arpeggios/scales from other tonalities to make new sounds.

Motif building

Motifs – short, well-formed melodic ideas that we take and develop – are the guitar soloist's storytelling device. We'll look at how to develop motifs, how to phrase well, leave space, and how to use motifs as the building blocks of a cohesive solo.

Chromaticism

Adding chromatic passing notes (i.e. notes from outside the key center) to scale shapes we already know, is a great way to play longer, flowing lines that come with in-built tension and release. We'll look at how to blend chromatic lines with more standard vocabulary, how to target chord tones to anchor the harmony, and how to apply sidestepping movements to create surprise "outside-inside" tensions.

Use of more colorful scales

It's easy to fall into using our favorite scales and patterns when soloing, but using other related scales can create much more interesting tensions. If, for instance, we're soloing over an Em7 vamp, we might naturally tend towards the E Blues scale or use E Minor Pentatonic ideas. But scales such as E Dorian, Melodic Minor and Harmonic Minor all yield a richer selection of colors, while still incorporating the classic pentatonic sound.

Articulation

Finally, we'll look at how to get the most out of the notes we play by adding bends and slides, playing saxophone-style unison note phrases, using legato technique, and applying soulful, emotive phrasing.

I hope you enjoy this exploration of how I approach this music, and I'm certain you'll learn some new ideas that grow and expand your guitar vocabulary.

Have fun!

Shane

Get the Audio

The audio files for this book are available to download for free from **www.fundamental-changes.com.** The link is in the top right-hand corner. Simply select this book title from the drop-down menu and follow the instructions to get the audio.

We recommend that you download the files directly to your computer, not to your tablet, and extract them there before adding them to your media library. You can then put them on your tablet or smart phone. On the download page, there is a help PDF, and we also provide technical support via the contact form.

For over 350 free guitar lessons with videos check out:

www.fundamental-changes.com

Join our free Facebook Community of Motivated Musicians

www.facebook.com/groups/fundamentalguitar

Tag us for a share on Instagram: **FundamentalChanges**

Warm-up Drills

The examples in the chapters that follow include some crosspicking and string-skipping ideas, as well as phrases that include passages of chromatic passing notes, especially in the later chapters. For that reason, I thought it would be useful to include here some of the picking drills I give to students who want to sharpen up their technique.

We can never spend too much time refining our picking technique – it's part of the mechanical process that enables us to play what we hear in our head. The following drills will help you warm up the picking/fretting hands, but also prepare you to play any kind of material you encounter. Spend some time on them now, and return here for a warm-up routine whenever you sit down to practice.

Picking practice tips

Always play to a metronome when practicing these drills. Working with the metronome will improve your sense of time while you are refining your technique. Start at a comfortable speed for the drill in question. There's no point setting an ambitious target speed then playing the drill poorly – all you'll be doing is learning to play badly faster! Don't practice a drill until you get it right, practice it until you can't get it wrong. Only then should you increase the tempo to challenge yourself.

These drills are purposely designed to test picking accuracy with some wide interval string skips. Stick with them and they will build your picking technique like nothing else, But this will take time, so be patient.

Use alternate picking throughout, beginning each exercise with a downstroke. Make it your aim to lock in with the metronome as tightly as possible. Use a light sounding click and see if you can make it "disappear" by playing tightly in time with it.

Picking drills

This first drill has been used many times in a variety of ways and was a staple of Berklee College tuition for many years. It's a crosspicking training exercise with chromatic notes that move across consecutive strings.

Begin on the sixth string, 1st fret, and play four chromatic notes with one finger per fret (beginning with the first finger on fret 1), then repeat the pattern across all strings.

When the pattern has been completed on the first string, move up one fret then descend the pattern, beginning with the fourth finger on the first string, 5th fret.

When that pattern is complete, move up one fret on the sixth string and repeat, and so on.

Continue up the fretboard until you finish the drill in 12th position. Focus on picking accuracy, producing each note clearly and cleanly, locking into the metronome. 80bpm is probably a good starting tempo but go slower if you need to and always favor accuracy and good technique over speed.

Drill 1

The second drill is a string-skipping exercise where the distance you are required to skip gets progressively wider. It's purposely an un-musical sounding drill because it's intended to test your picking accuracy and improve the mechanics of your technique and nothing else.

Think of the notes as being grouped in fours. Play the first two notes of each four-note group with the first and second fingers, and the subsequent two notes with the third and fourth fingers. Then move onto the next four-note group and repeat the fingering.

This is a challenge for the fretting hand as well as the picking hand, especially in bar three where the movement will probably feel unnatural to the fretting hand to begin with.

Drill 2

Here is another string-skipping exercise I like to use. In bar one, each note is picked twice, followed by a string skip and the pattern is played with straight 1/16th notes.

In bar two, we switch to playing 1/16th note triplets, requiring a *down-up-down* picking motion on each string. Then the whole pattern loops and repeats.

Try looping the pattern around several times and also move it to different areas of the fretboard.

Drill 3

The next drill uses a G major arpeggio arranged to include string skips. In a moment we're going to play the whole harmonized G Major scale across the neck using this pattern, so take a moment to familiarize yourself with it and memorize the pattern of consecutive and string-skipped notes.

Drill 4a

Now here is the full exercise. Work through it slowly and aim to play it smoothly. It's quite difficult to do this, so by all means break it down then build it back up. In other words, play bar one a few times, then add in bar two. Repeat bars 1-2 together several times. Now add in bar three and play bars 1-3 several times until you get the transitions between arpeggios sounding smooth and accurate.

Continue in this manner until you can play the whole exercise without making a mistake. Once you've mastered the shape and mechanics of it, then focus on playing it a little faster each practice session.

Drill 4b

With this brief warm-up done, let's move onto the music.

Chapter One – "Big Timer"

We're going to ease our way into things with a moody, modal vamp. My aim is to show you some vocabulary that works over single-chord vamps and bluesy progressions to begin with. As we move on, later chapters will feature tunes with more complex harmonies and the soloing ideas will become more advanced.

Funk comes in all shapes and sizes and this tune, with its slow-burning groove, allows us plenty of space to develop ideas. Once you've worked through the melodic ideas in this chapter, jam over the backing track and experiment by adding your own flavor to the music.

If you've not done so already, head over to **https://www.fundamental-changes.com/download-audio-choose-instrument/** and get the audio now!

Modal vamps are common in funk. The idea is that a tune will shift between tonal centers from different key signatures (in this case C Minor and Eb Minor) and the chords are usually of the same type.

This means we have to solo in two keys and find ways to smoothly connect our melodic ideas as we transition from one chord to the next. Our aim is to not allow the chord changes to get in the way of our melodic ideas, so that they sound forced. Instead, we want to express ourselves freely and flow over the top of the chords.

Cm11 and Ebm11 are a minor third interval away from each other (four frets on the guitar, including the C note) and this is a great interval to practice playing over as it crops up a lot in jazz-funk, as well as other musical styles.

In order to signal the chord changes, we'll often focus on hitting chord tones. But we want to do so in a seamless way without making awkward jumps on the fretboard. So, let's pause for a second and examine the two chords we're playing over.

Cm11 has the notes: C, Eb, G, Bb, D, F

Ebm11 has the notes: Eb, Gb, Bb, Db, F, Ab

Although these chords initially appear far apart and unrelated on the guitar fretboard, they actually have some useful things in common.

First, they share three chord tones. They both contain the notes Eb, Bb and F – they just represent different intervals in each chord. For example, Eb is the b3 of Cm11 and the root of Ebm11. We can use these notes to pivot between the two chords because they work over both.

Second, the notes that they *don't* have in common are all a half step apart. In other words, we only have to move a half step to go from the G of Cm11 to the Gb of Ebm11, or the C of Cm11 to the Db of Ebm11.

Spend some time considering these transition points.

It's important to start a solo with a confident opening statement and Example 1a makes use of repetition. The 11th interval of the C minor chord (F) is a cool tone, so we go straight for that and make it stand out. Bars 1-2 use the C Natural Minor scale (C, D, Eb, F, G, Ab, Bb) to form the melody.

In bar three here, we take the root note of the Cm11 chord and bend it up a half step shape to hit Db, the b7 of the Ebm11 chord.

Example 1a

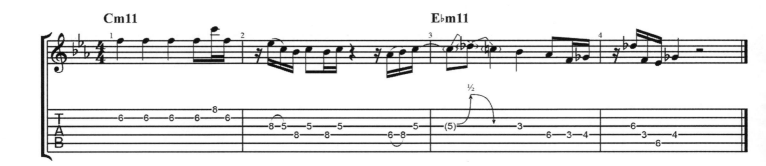

This line uses a question and answer phrase in bars 1-2. This simple idea used in the blues means we make a musical statement and follow it with a similar one, often in a different register on the guitar, so that it sounds like a conversation.

This line also uses a modal soloing idea. In bar one, we're using the C Natural Minor scale again, but bar two uses the C Dorian scale (C, D, Eb, F, G, A, Bb). C Dorian is the second mode in the key of Bb Major, which means at this point we're viewing the Cm11 as a ii chord, rather than the i chord, and playing an appropriate scale for it.

The takeaway here is to focus on what I call the "color note". This is the note that gives the scale its distinctive flavor or sound. In this case, it's the A note, the natural 6th. In my opinion, this is the approach that's often missing when people teach modes. Just focus on the color notes and get that sound in your head.

C Dorian only has one note different to C Natural Minor (A instead of Ab), but that one note really transforms the sound. If you've heard the tune *So What* by Miles Davis, it's full of Dorian phrases that produce a cool, dark sound. This is the color note.

To move from Cm11 to Ebm11, we use a half step movement as the G note at the end of bar two resolves to Ab at the beginning of bar three (the 11th of Ebm11). The notes over the Ebm11 chord can all be found in the Eb Minor Pentatonic scale.

Example 1b

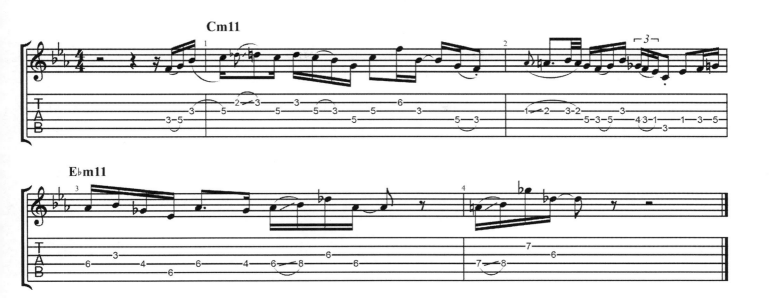

Be sure to listen to the audio for this next line before playing it. It's all about making the most of the bends and injecting emotion into the phrasing. Notice that there is a mix of whole step, half step and blues curl bends (the latter notated as a 1/4 bend, i.e. the note is just pushed slightly sharp).

Bar one uses the C Dorian scale again. To negotiate the change from Cm11 to Ebm11, play a whole step bend on the G string from the 10th to 12th fret to hit a G note, then release the bend and slide into the 13th fret (Ab). This movement is the 5th of Cm11 to the 11th of Ebm11.

Example 1c

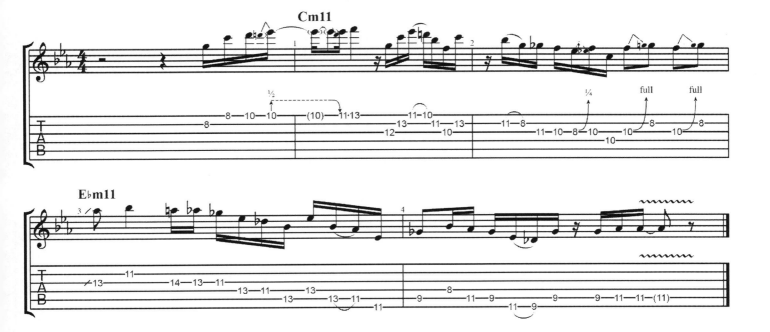

The next line begins with a more intervallic pattern. The first four notes spell out part of a standard C minor barre chord, but watch out for the quick jump up to the 13th fret on the first string. Play this line with economy picking, picking downward on the 5th string, 10th fret, then pushing downward through the rest of the strings without lifting the pick.

Wide intervals always add interest and surprise to a melodic line. In bar two, the phrase that begins on beat two alternates between the 7th and 11th frets. It also borrows the b5 note from the C Blues scale (Gb).

Listen to the audio to capture the feel of the line over Ebm11 in bars 3-4. Inject as much feeling as you can into the bends, especially in bar four where you need to bend to the note, control the pitch, then release it.

Example 1d

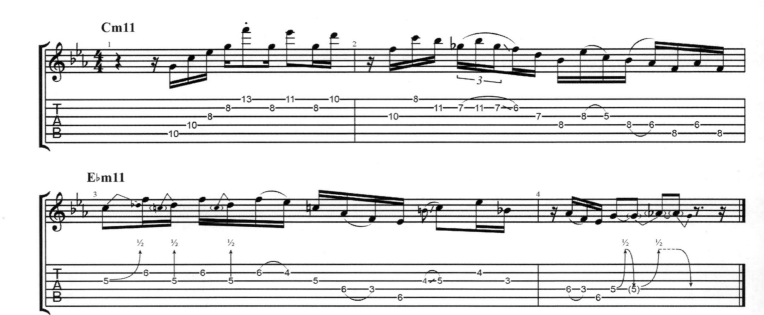

Over the Cm11 chord in this example, we play a sequenced pattern with some repeated notes. One thing we can do to make our lines more interesting is to play a familiar scale pattern but "borrow" a note from a related scale to augment it. Here we take the C Natural Minor scale but add in the b5 note (Gb) from the C Blues scale to form a hybrid pattern that has more of an edge to its sound. Try experimenting with this on your own and see what licks you can create by adding in the b5 note.

I should add that I mostly think in terms of chords and chord tones when soloing, rather than entire scales, but it's important for you to be familiar with both at first. When you get more experience and begin to master phrasing, you will naturally find your own path to choosing strong notes and phrases.

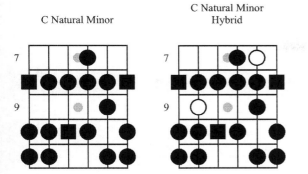

Example 1e

In bars 1-2 of this line, we use the C Blues scale, starting low on the neck and transitioning into the higher register via a position slide on the fourth string. Make this shift by playing a C note on the third string, before sliding into a C note on the fourth string, 10th fret. This is an idea borrowed from saxophonists, who refer to it as *double tonguing*. On guitar, the idea is to play the same note in quick succession but on different strings to give it a different timbre.

In bars 3-4 we're using the Eb Natural Minor scale to create this simple phrase. Be careful to control your bends and strive for accurate pitching on the bent notes.

Example 1f

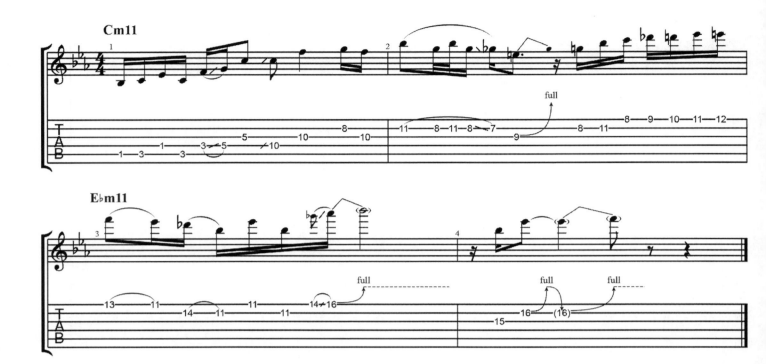

The next lick has a picking challenge for you. To avoid simply running up and down scale patterns, breaking up patterns into wider intervals creates much more interest and a melodic surprise to the listener's ears. Here you need to pick the notes on the fourth string, then quickly jump to the first string to play a quick hammer-on. The pattern moves sequentially down the C Natural Minor scale until we run out of frets.

After playing this phrase, execute a quick change of position to play the phrase over the Ebm11 chord, which uses the Eb Natural Minor scale.

Example 1g

Here's the final section of the solo. In the pickup bar, this phrase is played over the Ebm11 chord, but the lick is a complete idea that flows into the Cm11 chord that follows in bar one. The first four notes spell out an Ebm6 arpeggio, then we immediately shift into C Dorian to anticipate the Cm11.

In bar one, the half step bend from an A note targets the b7 (Bb) of Cm11. This long bend is echoed in bar three over Ebm11, where a whole step bend from Eb targets the 9th (F) of the chord. The line ends with another intervallic descending scale sequence.

Example 1h

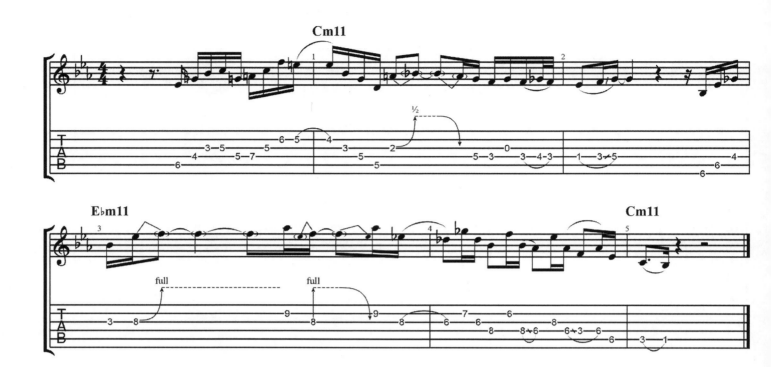

You've practiced every section of the solo, so now have a listen to the audio of the complete solo, then work at joining all the parts together. And, of course, just have fun jamming over the backing track.

Chapter Two – "Slow"

In this chapter we're going to learn some soloing ideas over another slow-burning tune, this time with a gospel feel. After the simple chord structures used in Chapter One, this tune called *Slow* (from my solo record *The Grease Factor*) has richer chord changes that include some altered dominant chords. This makes it really fun to solo over. This is the actual track from the recording that I've used here for this lesson.

After learning a complete solo, we'll also look at how we might approach this tune rhythmically and learn a complete rhythm guitar part that has some cool ideas you can steal and adapt.

Soloing approaches

For this type of music, bluesy emotive phrases work really well, because gospel music has to be played with a soulful vibe. We're in the key of C and we ease our way into the tune with a laid-back C Minor Pentatonic lick.

A common approach in the blues is to freely mix minor and major pentatonic scales over chords that are played as dominant 7s. C Minor Pentatonic has the notes C, Eb, F, G, Bb, and the C7 chord is constructed C, E, G, Bb. However, the Eb which could be considered a clashing note turns into a cool #9 tone to imply a C7#9 harmony. Here, the #9 is highlighted all the more by the fact that we bend into it from a half step below and hold it.

For the A7#5 chord, we play another half step bend to target the 3rd (C#) of the chord. Bending to a chord tone from a half step below is a simple idea, but it's ear catching and creates a little moment of tension.

Example 2a

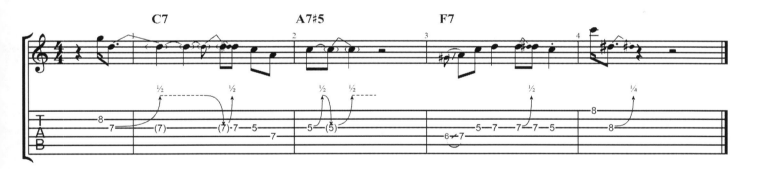

The next example begins with the same idea, transferred onto the first string. Over C7, the D note is bent a half step to Eb for that #9 sound. We spell out the A7#5 with a 6ths phrase (*a la* Steve Cropper) using the 5th and the 3rd of the chord (E, C#). Throughout this lick, aim for a "lazy" phrasing feel and play behind the beat. Guitar players can tend to play too fast, so if you think you're playing it too lazily, you're probably spot on!

In bars 3-4, this line is based around the F Mixolydian scale but I'm also using the idea of approaching an F7 chord tone from a half step below (the G# to A movement which occurs in both bars). If you've never experimented with this before, there are some cool licks to be found by playing half step approach notes below each note of a triad.

Example 2b

A new chord appears in bar two this time around. A dominant 7#11 chord is technically a five-note chord. The chord F#7 has the notes F#, A#, C# and E. We keep all those notes then add the #11 (a C note) to make F#7#11, but because five-note chords can be tricky to arrange on guitar, often the natural 5th is left out.

If this chord seems like a harmonic curveball to you, try playing the following set of chord voicings (the F/G chord will appear at the beginning of Example 2d):

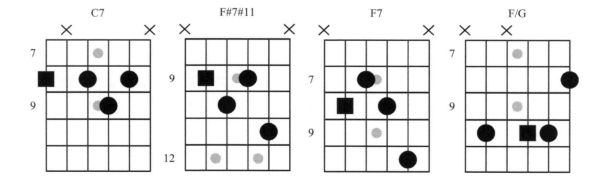

The F#7#11 chord is being used as a chromatic approach chord in the same way we might use a chromatic approach note. We could make a feature of this chord by playing some kind of altered scale over it, but we can also use a simpler parent scale from the key signature and allow those notes to create their own tensions. In bar one, the lick over C7 is minor pentatonic in nature but has several passing notes added in. We continue the C Minor Pentatonic phrasing in bar two.

Example 2c

Over blues-based tunes made up of dominant chords, we always have a number of scale choices. Blues players will always blur the harmony by playing both minor and major ideas. Over the C7 chord, C Minor or Major Pentatonic, the C Blues scale, and C Mixolydian are all options. Here, we're playing a C Major Pentatonic idea and backpedaling through the scale.

Example 2d

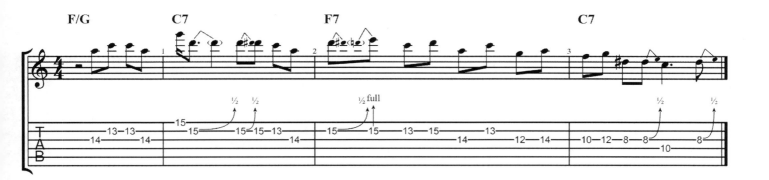

In Example 2e, in bar one I'm moving between a C major triad and a C7 arpeggio that begins with a b5 note.

Another way of looking at this idea is the thinking used by jazz guitarists like Pat Martino and Wes Montgomery. Both often "superimposed" a minor arpeggio or scale a perfect 5th interval above a dominant 7 chord. A perfect 5th above C is G, and this idea could be interpreted as using the G Melodic Minor scale, which contains all of the notes.

I prefer to think in terms of chord tones, but if you like to use scales and you've never thought of using an idea like this in your solos, spend some time learning the G Melodic Minor scale, then put on a C7 chord loop (there are plenty on YouTube) and jam over it. There are some cool licks to be found in there.

Example 2e

Let's try that idea again but this time over the A7#5 chord (because it works just as well over altered dominant chords). A perfect 5th above A is E, so this time we'll use the E Melodic Minor scale (E, F#, G, A, B, C#, D#) to form the melody.

When you learn this example, be sure to listen to the audio beforehand. In bars 3-4 it's important to nail the articulation with those slides.

Example 2f

We often think of bending notes on the high strings, but not so much on the low strings, yet this can sound dramatic. In bar one, play a blues curl on the fourth string, 1st fret, to push the D# note towards the 3rd (E) of C7.

In bar two here, we ignore the passing chord harmony and creating a riff based on moving a fragment of F7 backward and forward a half step.

Example 2g

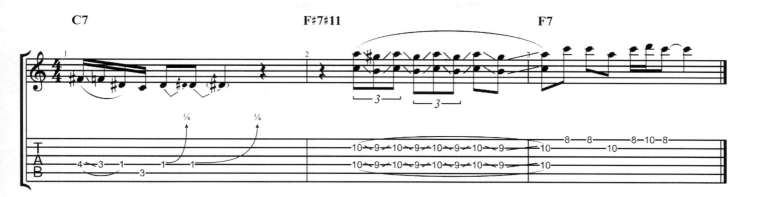

After playing some complex harmonic ideas, it's always good to bring things back to the blues by way of contrast. Here's a C Major Pentatonic line with some expressive bends. For the A7#5 chord, at the end of bar two we bend a note to target the 5th of the chord. Focus on bending accuracy and make this series of bends as expressive as possible. The double-stop bend in bar three, however, is more about the feel that pitch accuracy, as it's meant to be slurred.

Example 2h

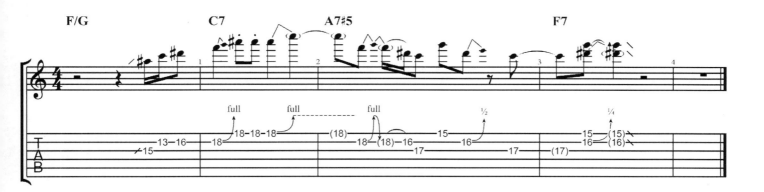

The next idea begins with a descending run using the notes of the C Blues scale. Bend the note on the second string, 16th fret, with your third finger, reinforced by your other fingers. After playing the next two notes, begin the legato phrase from the first string, 13th fret, with your first finger. It's a quick, flowing line, so work out your fretting/picking hand coordination beforehand.

In bar two, execute another low string bend to target the 5th of the A7 chord. Note that we're bending to the note E, as if the chord was a regular A7, ignoring the #5. This is fine to do and just creates a little extra tension.

In bar three, we use the C Blues scale to finish the line. You may notice that I made a small addition to the scale. Throughout this lick, but especially in bar three, I added an A note, which is not in the C Blues scale. Let me take a moment to explain the thinking behind this.

Remember what I said about color notes and finding a note to add a new flavor to a scale? To achieve a more modern sound, we take the basic C Minor Pentatonic scale, which has the notes C, Eb, F, G, Bb and swap out the b7 (Bb) for a major 6th (A). This gives us the C Minor Six Pentatonic scale: C, Eb, F, G, A. It keeps the bluesy-ness of the original scale, but adds a cooler, sophisticated edge.

Use an app or an online fretboard map to lay out that scale across the fretboard and experiment with it, because it's a cool sound.

Often, I'll just play the minor six pentatonic scale straight, but here I also wanted the b5 sound from the blues scale, so borrowed that note to create another hybrid scale.

This idea works well over the C7 chord, but equally well over the F7.

Example 2i

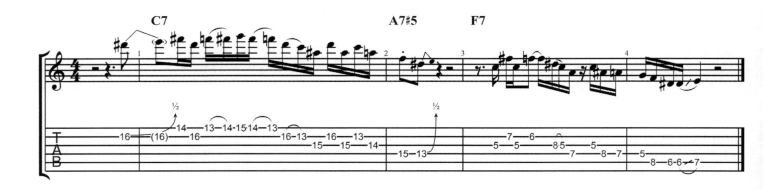

Now for the longest and most complex idea in the solo. It's a continuous line, so I needed to show you the whole seven-bar idea in full, but you can break it down into smaller chunks to learn it.

The first idea is an ascending motif in bars 1-2. The G note on the fourth string, 5th fret, is the anchor or pedal tone for this line. Starting with an E note, play half step movements with hammer-ons/pull-offs that ascend the neck, one fret at a time. Some of the movements sound inside and some outside, but the G anchor note holds it all together.

This lick transitions onto the second string and then we pause on a C# note on the third string, 6th fret. This is the 5th of the F#7#11 chord. After a rest, the line continues until we hit an Eb note on beat 1 of bar three, over the F7 chord (b7). The whole line makes sense because we began on one strong chord tone and we're ending on another. As long as we keep a clear target in mind, we can take some liberties with the notes in between.

In bar three, the first four notes of the ascending run over F7 are the F Minor Pentatonic scale. The next four spell an F major triad – or you could think of this as switching between F Minor and F Major Pentatonic scales.

In bar four, the chord is F/G (an F major triad over a G bass note). You can think of this chord as a hipper sounding F7 or sus chord.

We ended the ascending run on an F note and, launching from this, we descend chromatically on the top two strings. Bars 5-6 are all about bending into strong chord tones. Bar seven ends with a classic rock lick.

Practice the ideas we've discussed separately, then begin to combine them until you've got the whole thing down.

Example 2j

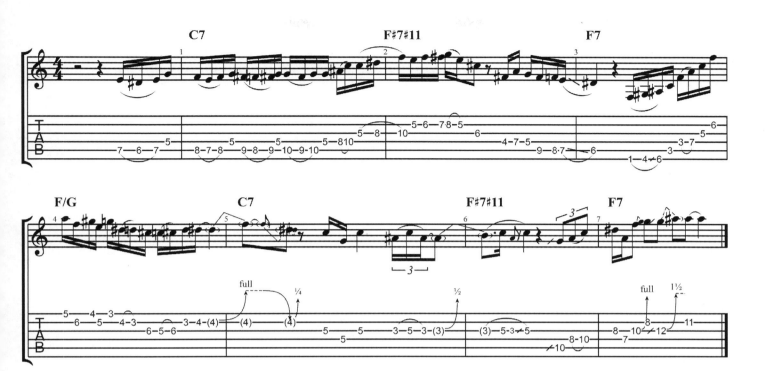

In this final example, the tune draws to a close with a classic gospel ending. In bar one, we play a simple C Minor Pentatonic lick. In bar two, another name for the chord Bbm/Eb is Eb7sus2 and here we could play a melody from either a Bb minor or an Eb dominant tonality. I opted for the latter and played a bluesy lick with passing notes based around an Eb7 chord in 11th position.

Listen to the audio and you'll hear that the chords in the final two bars suggest an overall major tonality for this section, so for this lick I used the C Major scale with a couple of added passing notes.

Example 2k

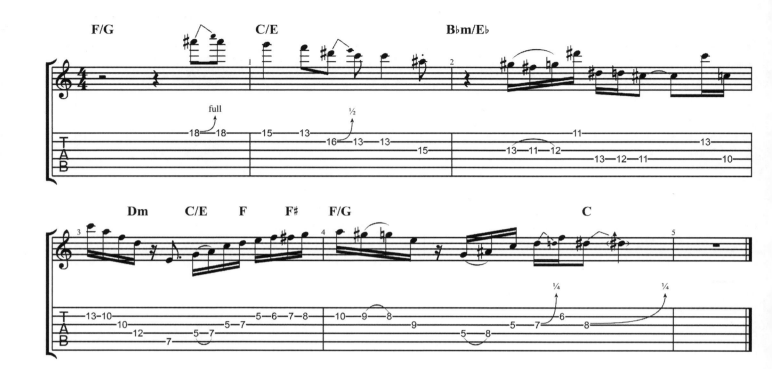

Rhythm approaches

Nearly all guitar players enjoy taking a solo, but we should never underestimate the power of a well-constructed rhythm part to really lift a tune. For the rest of this chapter, we're going to look at some creative ideas to play a complete rhythm guitar part for this track.

The aim of these ideas is to create a soulful, laid-back vibe, where we really feel the music, and seek to add a little syncopation and funkiness. To do that, we'll draw on ideas from RnB and soul. This means mixing up chordal ideas with double-stops, 6ths, and a few single-note ideas. I'll also show you some nice chord voicings used by the pioneers of RnB.

The opening example contains some of all of that, so let's break it down!

First, here's a nice alternative to a standard C7. If we take the 3rd of the chord (E) on the third string and move it down a whole step, while the other notes remain the same, we get a C7sus2 chord.

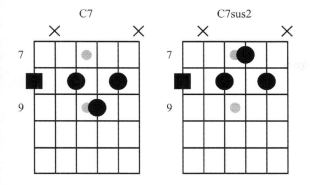

It still captures the essence of C7 but has a more open sound. Slide it back and forth a whole step to span bars one and two. This idea is more about feel than accuracy.

A simple idea we can use is to rhythmically displace the bass note from the upper part of a chord. In bar three, we use a standard F7 voicing but play the upper structure and the bass note off each other (adding some palm muting to the bass) and this gives the chord a funky feel.

Another important tool for playing New Orleans style soul or gospel appears in bar four. The idea here is to spell out the sound of C7 very simply with 6ths. There is always a string in between a 6th interval on guitar, so you can play this fingerstyle, with hybrid picking, or just with a pick, though the latter is tricky unless you're very adept at string muting.

To elevate this idea into something more interesting, we can slide in and out of 6ths that contain C7 chord tones. Play this idea as lazily as possible – it's better if it's not strictly to tempo, so that it floats over the groove.

In the final bar we have a single note idea. At the end of the bar, just push the b7 of the chord (Eb) slightly sharp with a blues curl to add a bit of tension.

Example 21

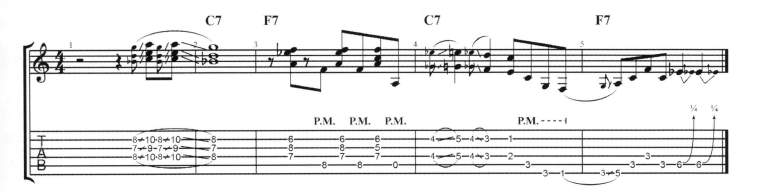

In the next section, we take the idea of rhythmically displacing the bass notes from the upper structures to create a syncopated rhythm that moves between C7 and F7.

The first chord here is an alternative voicing of C7sus2. The chord that follows in bar one is a little unusual. Thought of in relation to the C7 harmony, it's a C7sus4 with an added 9th. If that sounds too mind-boggling, we know from our previous discussion that G minor sounds can work over C7, so we can think of both chords as essentially Gm over a C bass.

The opening chord lick combines palm muting and slides in a James Brown kind of way, so be sure to get this sounding tight.

The syncopation and position shift is tricky in bar two. Rather than finger a full F7 chord here, you can just barre the 1st fret with your first finger, and at the end of the bar play the 3rd fret notes with the third finger. Then, you need to quickly jump your fretting up to play an A7 at the beginning of bar three that slides up to a C7.

RnB rhythm parts make great use of chord fragments – stripped-down chords that make the desired sound without the need for cumbersome barre chords. On beat 3 of bar three, the first fragment is from a C9 chord. Both the root and the 5th have been left out, so we end up with a cool 9th, 3rd and b7 voicing (from low to high). The fragment that follows is from a C6 chord. Play a C bass note, then these two chords and I'm sure you'll have heard this sound in countless RnB recordings. You can start with the C6 fragment and hammer onto the C9.

The idea ends with an Fadd9 chord.

Example 2m

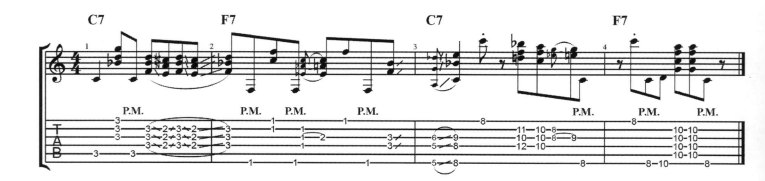

There are no new ideas to discuss here, just more syncopation and sliding practice. In bar three, we change the A7 to an A13 to add more color, and in bar four we combine an F7sus2 voicing with an F13 (with the root on top) to give the F dominant sound some contrast, moving to a regular F7 in bar five.

Example 2n

This example is a syncopation workout for you. Most of the time in this idea, we avoid playing the chords on the beat. We're using chord forms you're familiar with, so focus on nailing the rhythms. Have a careful listen to the accompanying audio track. Palm mute the bass notes and play the upper chord structures with a tight, staccato feel.

Example 2o

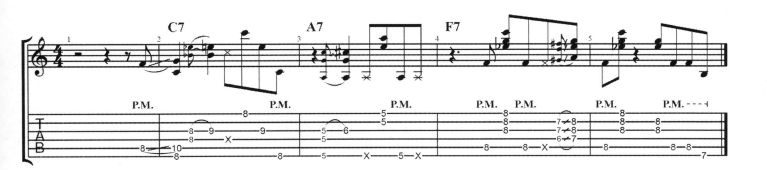

In this example, the rhythm part is really broken up, with all the bass notes displaced from the upper chord structures. Aim to play it in tight, funky way, applying palm muting. Hold down the chord shapes throughout. Most of the time they are simple three-note shapes. Work on your timing to really make this pop.

Example 2p

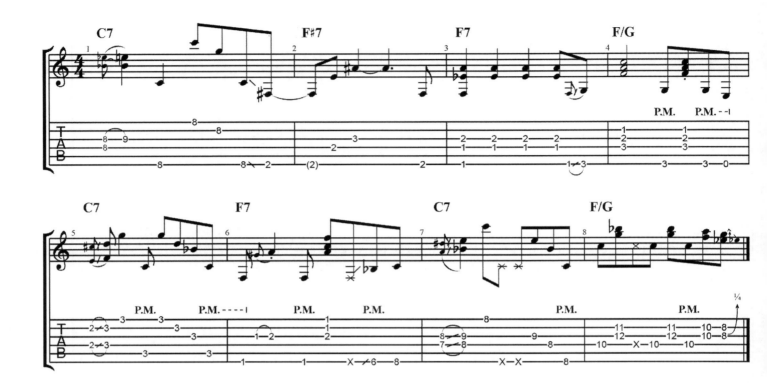

After the busyness of the previous idea, we begin this part of the tune playing more sparsely, adding some sliding articulation. Bar five has a bluesy lick around the C7 chord which should be a nice addition to your chord-lick ideas. Play the sliding 6ths with your second and third fingers, keeping the first finger free to play the G note on the first string. After the slide down, slip into a three-note C7 voicing at the 3rd fret.

In bar five, you'll end up fretting the C7 chord with your second finger on the fifth string, 3rd fret. For the A7 chord in bar six, slide the second finger up one fret to play the note at the 4th. On the fourth string, it's easiest to play the note at the 2nd fret with the first finger, then allow the third finger to take over and execute the slide up to the 5th. Your first finger will then move over a string to play the third string, 2nd fret. Keep fretting the previous note so that they ring together.

Example 2q

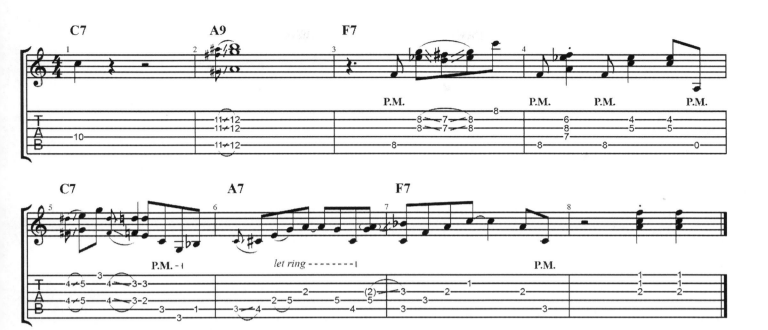

In bar six of this line, use your third finger to slide up to the 12th fret on the fifth string, and your first finger to play the 10th fret partial barre. Slide down to the 8th fret and stretch for the 12th fret note on the fifth string with your fourth finger. After playing the two-note F7 voicing, use the fourth finger again to play the note on the 10th fret. Slide back and forth in a laid-back style in bar seven.

Example 2r

33

Here's a cool chordal lick with a couple of ideas I think you might enjoy!

First, in bar three, this idea is built around the F9 chord shape below at the 13th fret. The F root note on the sixth string is left out and we use the A note on the fifth string for rhythmic displacement instead. Played without its root, the chord shape looks like an Am7b5.

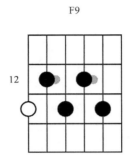

To play the lick in bar four, release your first and second fingers from the chord. The third and fourth fingers will be holding the remaining two notes, which you'll slide up from the 13th to 15th fret. Use the first finger to play the note on the top string.

The second main idea here is the use of multiple chord fragments to create a chord-lick over the C7 and A7 chords in bars 5-6.

In bar five, we start with a C7 mini-chord that omits the root and uses the 5th, b7 and 3rd. The fragment we slide into at the 10th is part of a Csus4, and the third chord is a simple C major triad. As we hop over onto the next string set, the fourth chord is part of a C7sus4. The two notes at the 10th fret imply a C6.

In bar six, we begin by playing a straight A major triad twice. This is followed by an A7sus2, then an A6. Finally, an A6sus4 resolves to a straight A major chord.

Although I've taken some time to explain the chord fragment voicings for the curious, don't worry about the chords too much. It's better to memorize this idea as a sequence of chord shapes that work around a particular position on the neck. This way, you'll find it easier to move the idea around and play it in other keys.

Example 2s

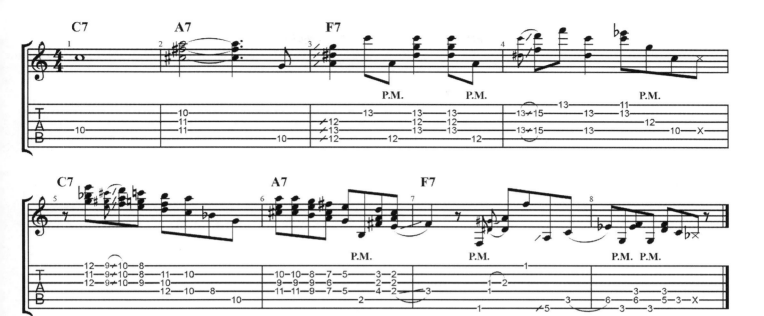

As we come to a close, this section opens with the C7sus2 voicing we've used throughout. When we reach the C/E chord in bar six, the chord shape might resemble an Em7b5 to you, but it's just a C9 chord with the sixth string root omitted. To end the rhythm part, we just follow what the bass and keys are doing on the backing track, climbing chromatically on the fifth string.

Example 2t

I hope you enjoyed learning some RnB-style rhythm over this tune. Put on the backing track and test out your chord licks, as well as practicing the solo!

Chapter Three – "F Thing!"

We couldn't explore this genre of music without looking at a tune that has a New Orleans style funk groove, and that's where the tune *F Thing!* comes in. This tune is from my record *Still Motion* and again I've borrowed the rhythm track from the actual recording for our lesson here.

This tune is a blues in F but has a couple of chord variations thrown in to change it up a little. It also has an unusual tag at the end of each chorus, one bar of 2/4. This idea keeps us on our toes because it disrupts the usual pattern of the blues with a "reset" and means we need to count it well to know where we are. Here's the structure:

| F | % | % | % |

| Bb7 | Ab7 | F | % |

| C7 | Eb7 | F | F Bb |

Plus 1 x 2/4 bar to turn the progression around.

In this chapter we'll explore some ideas you can use to freshen up your blues playing, such as sidestepping and superimposing pentatonic patterns.

The solo kicks off with an F Minor Pentatonic idea. Pick the opening double-stop with a hard attack and push the notes slightly sharp. We continue with the pentatonic feel in bar two, but in bar three spell out the sound of the F7 chord. F Minor Pentatonic contains an Ab note, but playing an A here (the 3rd of F7) is enough to imply F7.

In the previous chapter, we discussed the jazz concept of playing in a minor tonality a perfect 5th above a dominant chord and bar four uses this idea. A perfect 5th above F is C, and the first five notes come from a Cm9 arpeggio. The last four notes come from visualizing an F9 chord with its root on the fifth string, 8th fret. They are all within easy reach of that shape.

The last four notes of bar four become a short motif for the solo, so we follow that up with two more four-note phrases. Some more chordal thinking is applied over the Bb7 chord, and this four-note phrase begins on the #5 of the chord.

The pentatonic phrase spanning bars 7-8 requires some precise fingering. It begins with a half step bend that you should be able to play with just your second finger, then play the first string, 11th fret, with your first finger. As soon as you've played the second bend (or even while you're playing it) move your first finger to play the 9th fret on the second string. You should now be in position to play the rest of the run. You should end up with your first finger on the third string, 8th fret, at the end of bar seven, then reach over and bend the fifth string, 11th fret with your third finger. You can keep fretting the third string with the first finger to allow the notes to resonate.

Example 3a

As this tune is in the key of F with a dominant chord feel, the F Mixolydian scale is a good choice for soloing. In bar one, even though we're soloing over C7, F Mixolydian works perfectly well. We continue with this mode in bar two over the Eb7 chord. Though it might not seem like an obvious choice, the notes of F Mixolydian (F, G, A, Bb, C, D, Eb) contain some chord tones of Eb7, plus a bunch of interesting extended or altered notes.

Bar three has a pedal tone idea, with a high F note as its anchor point. After playing the notes at the 11th/12th fret on the fifth string, you can barre with your first finger at the 13th fret to play this lick, and you'll probably find it easiest to play it fingerstyle due to the wide interval,

Example 3b

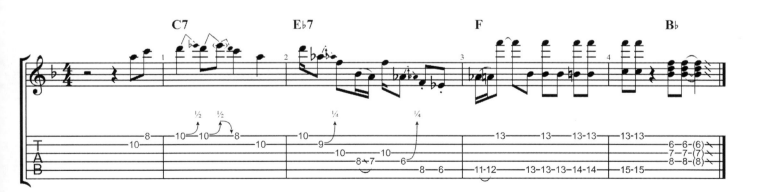

This example begins with the 2/4 breakdown bar, so the phrasing may sound a little unusual the first time you listen to the audio. The first note of the lick is played on beat 2 of the pickup bar.

The ascending line is a spread-out F major triad played over two octaves and is played with a triplet feel, which cuts against the straight marching groove of the drums. This adds to the phrasing challenge! Rather than trying to count the line, the best approach is to listen to it several times and just feel the timing.

In bars 3-4, this lick continues to play with the rhythmic feel. Technically, the phrase isn't too hard to play – it's an F Mixolydian scale idea, organized in a way that gives it a pentatonic shape – but the notes are arranged in groups of five, with no rest in between.

To play the sequence, fret the fourth and third string notes at the 8th and 10th frets with the first and third fingers. The first time through the sequence, play the second string, 11th fret, with your pinkie. The second time through the sequence, play the second string, 10th fret, by rolling your third finger onto it. Rather than frying your brain trying to count it, listen to the audio and learn it by feel.

Example 3c

The beginning of Example 3d is a continuation of the previous lick, as it ends and moves on to a new idea. In bar one we repeat the pentatonic style run up, then target the b7 (Ab) of the Bb7 chord, pushing it slightly sharp with a blues curl. The whole line is framed around F Mixolydian.

Example 3d

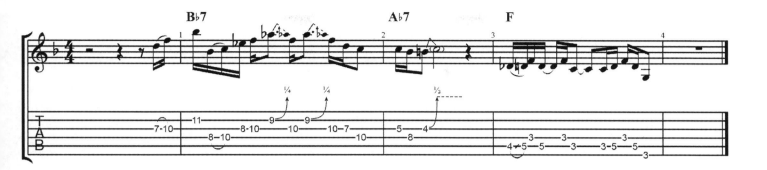

Next is a straight up blues-rock style lick. We anticipate the C7 chord by hitting the first double-stop on beat 4& of the pickup bar, then play the 5th and 3rd chord tones. Then we drop down to the 8th fret to play the root and 5th.

For the Eb7 chord we're hitting the 3rd and root note, then dropping down to the exact same shape as for the C7. The notes have a different effect over Eb7 and imply the sound of Eb13.

Example 3e

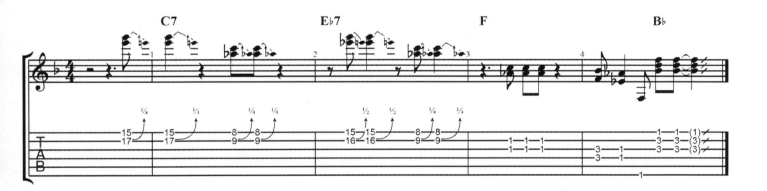

The next four bars feature a unison note saxophone style lick. On the third string, we play Eb to F, then the F note on the second string for the unison effect.

There are two ways to play this idea. If you prefer, you can hold down the second string F note with your first finger, and the third string Eb note with your second finger. Keep those notes fretted and hammer onto the F note on the third string, 10th fret, with your pinkie.

The way I do it is using economy picking, playing the first two notes with a single upstroke, and the next two notes with a sweeping downward pick stroke.

For this approach, keep your first finger anchored on the second string, 6th fret. On the third string, play the 8th fret with your second finger using an upstroke and the 10th with your pinkie but using a downstroke, then use the same downstroke motion to hit the F on the 2nd string, 6th fret. From there, begin the motion again with the upstroke.

Example 3f

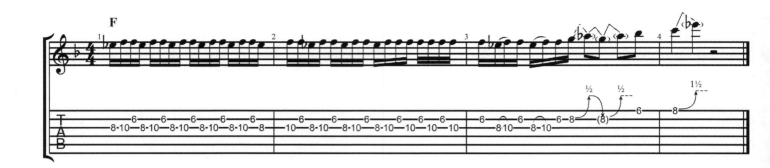

This idea uses 6ths to create a melodic idea around the Bb7 chord in bar one. It's a common RnB lick, but I added a little twist. I approached the first note of each 6ths shape from a half step below. This creates a nice tension and it's a fun lick to play.

Here, we're aiming for the Bb root note on the top string that falls on beat 4. However, we play a B note, creating tension, and hold it for a quarter note. The effect is magnified by the fact that we play the B on a downbeat (beat 2).

In bar two, I'm visualizing an Ab7 barre chord and playing notes around it. The resulting line spells an Ab triad in the first part of the bar.

Example 3g

To finish the tune, we end with another rhythmic line mostly driven by 1/8th note triplets, though in the first bar there is a slurred phrase that combines 1/16th and 1/8th notes. In bar one, after sliding into the third string, 15th fret, at the end of the pickup bar, rather than play the first four note phrase with alternate picking, I quickly drag my pick upward across the strings and slur all the notes. It's more about the sound it creates than picking/note accuracy.

For the note choices in this lick, I'm using the minor six pentatonic scale again.

F Minor Pentatonic has the notes F, Ab, Bb, C, Eb. If we replace the b7 (Eb) with a major 6th we get:

F, Ab, Bb, C, D.

We can't do justice to this scale's potential in one lick but do experiment with this sound in your practice times.

Example 3h

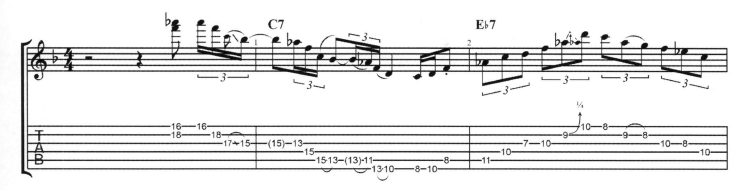

Now jam along to the backing track and have a go at the full solo.

Chapter Four – "Minor Bluesish"

During the early part of my career, I was fortunate enough to work with the Neville Brothers (also known as the "first family of funk") – icons of the New Orleans music scene. The eight years I spent with them played an important part in the way I approach playing music to this day.

They formed their band in New Orleans back in the late '70s and, drawing inspiration from the music of the region, and were instrumental in defining the sound of funk. *Minor Bluesish* is a nod towards the slow-burning, moody side of their music – a minor blues in the key of G Minor.

In this chapter, we're going to look at the idea of how to create musical motifs, so that our solos tell a story.

Motifs are short melodic ideas that repeat. They can be licks or melodic phrases of any length and are a great way of creating continuity in a solo, where we can use them to connect ideas. There are two ways we can use motifs:

First, we can play a phrase then repeat it note for note. Repetition is an important feature of the blues, and this can be a cool approach, where the motif has a different harmonic effect over different chords.

A second, more common, approach is to play a motif then adapt it. We can alter it to make it better fit a chord change (often by changing just one note), or we can develop the musical idea, using the motif as our starting point.

The "call and response" phrasing of the blues is the latter kind of motif development and really helps to establish a strong theme for a solo. This is the approach I've taken with the line in Example 4a. The motif is stated in the pickup bar/bar one and repeated in a lower register in bar two. All the notes come from the G Minor Pentatonic scale.

Example 4a

The next idea is a rhythmic motif. Note choices are always important, but we shouldn't underestimate the power of a strong rhythm to make a compelling musical statement. The simple idea here is to keep a similar rhythm going throughout, while we descend a G minor scale sequence. The idea also uses doubled-up notes, which helps the motif stand out all the more.

Example 4b

Motifs are a great tool for connecting ideas. If we take an idea then develop it, then develop it a little more, we take the listener on a journey. Focus on this area of your playing and you'll soon move beyond simply playing licks, and your solos will take on a whole new purpose.

In the next part of the solo, as the progression moves to Cm7, we take the previous motif and develop it. Notice that the rhythm and timing have changed a little, but the way the notes interact on the third and second strings continues. This is what creates the sense that the musical theme is continuing.

In bars 1-4, the note choices come from the G Natural Minor scale. In bar five, over the Gm7 chord, the first two notes highlight the 5th and b3 of the chord and then, to create a moment of tension, the D note is lowered to Db to make a b5 sound before we continue with notes from the minor scale.

Example 4c

Over the next four bars of G minor, we begin with some repetitive blues phrasing with G Minor Pentatonic. For the descending phrase in bar two, we switch to the G Natural Minor scale. If you play the first string hammer ons with your first and third fingers, and the note on the second string, 11th fret, with your fourth finger, you'll be in position to play the descending run, with the notes bouncing off the third string F pedal tone.

Example 4d

For the next part of the solo, I wanted to include some emotive bends that suited the minor feel of the piece. You'll notice that there is one bend in every bar, and this provides a kind of theme for the line. Half step bends in a minor key can conjure up a wistful emotion and are a little harder to control than full step bends, so they demand pitch accuracy.

Every bend here is targeting a chord tone. In the pickup bar/bar one we bend to Bb (the b7 of Cm7). Listen to the audio for this, as the release of this bend down to a G note (5th) is an important part of the phrase. In bar two, we bend to Eb (b3), and in bar three play a whole step bend up to a D (the 9th, for a Cm9 sound).

In bar four, the chord changes to the V chord, D7, and here the bend targets an F# note (3rd).

Think of the bends in this line as *anchor points* for the harmony, around which the other ideas are built.

Example 4e

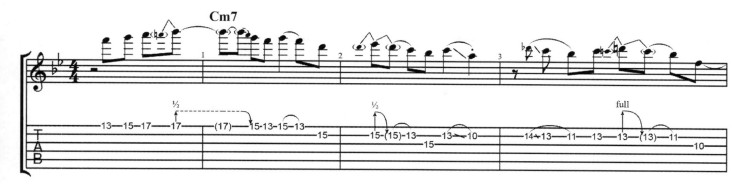

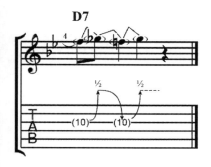

Next is a more intervallic idea, to create some contrast with the emotive bluesy phrasing. The use of 1/8th note triplets throughout is a way of making the line stand out, as it cuts against the marching 4/4 groove.

Let's look at the note choices here. In the pickup bar, a simple D major triad makes the sound of the D7 chord. It's pretty easy to spot that these notes are part of a 5th fret D major barre chord, but we're omitting the bass note.

In bar one, however, the three notes played on the 4th fret are *not* part of a Gm7 barre chord. Here, we're using a *sidestepping* technique.

The idea is to take a lick or pattern and move it up or down a half step on the fretboard, then back. Moving a lick or scale pattern in this way immediately creates an "outside" sound, which we resolve by moving it back into position.

You might think that moving a lick up/down a half step would result in every note being "wrong" i.e. chromatic, but this isn't always the case. The movement often results in a combination of other scale tones related to the chord, as well as chromatic notes.

Here, we're approaching the Gm7 chord from a half step above, playing outside, then immediately bringing it inside. Once we are back inside the harmony, the notes at the 5th fret create a Gsus4 sound.

Example 4f

Example 4g begins with some saxophone style unison notes, with an F note played on the second and third strings. Bar four utilizes the sidestepping technique again, as the middle group of notes spell out a G# minor chord, which slips back into G minor at the end of the bar. You can probably hear the melodic potential of this simple idea to create lines that sound more complex than they really are.

Example 4g

Here's a short idea that combines bends with double-stops over the Cm7 chord. In bars 2-3, the idea is to play a descending line that links together chord fragments in 6ths. You can look at this idea in two ways: all the notes can be found in the G Natural Minor scale, but they also belong to the C Dorian scale. I prefer to look at it as C Dorian as it helps me to "see" the chord tones as I approach the chord change. You can tell a great improviser by the way they outline the chord changes and create melodies within the progression, so it should always be your aim to be aware of the chord tones.

At the end of this line, we use the idea of bending into the F# chord tone of D7 and do so with a less common low string bend.

Example 4h

The next idea is a bridging line. After a bluesy line over Gm7, we leave some space, then launch into an expressive bend. Leaving a breath in the music, and playing something in the lower register, then the higher register, is a way of signaling to the listener that one idea is ending and another one is about to begin. It's just like taking a pause in a conversation before changing topic.

Think about how you like to apply vibrato on a bend. Vibrato is a technique that's often very personal to a player. On this lick, I apply a fast and fairly wide vibrato, the effect of which is to make it sound a little like slide guitar. You will have your own preferences, but be open to experimentation, as the articulation you use can make a big difference to the sound of a lick.

Example 4i

Example 4j uses a mix of approaches to create the melodic line and shows how we can construct an interesting line with a bit of creativity.

First of all, the high register phrase and bend echo the short motif that was stated at the end of the previous example. Then we have a descending run in bars 2-3 that uses the G Blues scale.

In bar four, for a change of musical mood, we turn to the G Melodic Minor scale for the first time in this tune. This scale shares five notes in common with G Natural Minor, but has a major 6th (E instead of Eb) and a major 7th (F# instead of F). Those two notes give the melodic minor its characteristic sound and after playing pentatonic and blues ideas, the lick in this bar immediately sounds more sophisticated.

Example 4j

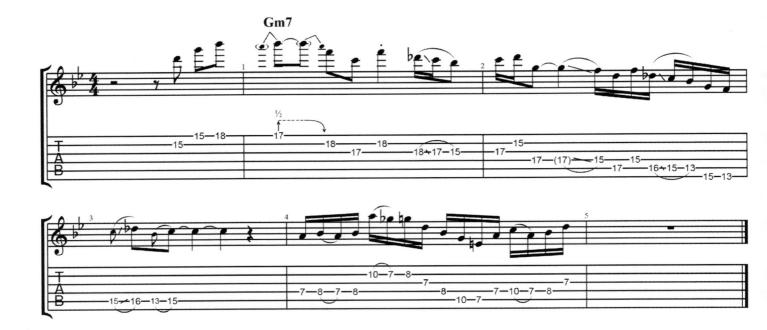

Next, we move on to another rhythmic motif. In the first three bars, the notes don't have much in common with each other, but the rhythmic phrasing is similar, and this ties the ideas together. In bar four, an ascending run in C Natural Minor contains a passing approach note at the end to target the G root note in bar five.

Example 4k

This example begins with another bending idea where the release of the bend is just as important as the upward motion. Controlling the release of a bend is something of a neglected art among guitar players! Then we move into a double-stop passage.

At the end of bar four, going into bar five is a triplet idea that needs some explanation.

The idea starts in a G minor chord shape then, as it ascends, we allow notes on adjacent strings to ring into each other. The notes that ring are ones that would sound dissonant if played normally at the same time: Bb and C, D and E – both a whole step apart. Played in this way, however, it has a pleasing effect.

You need to use a specific fingering to achieve this. In the second half of bar four, play the two notes at the 5th fret with the first finger. Play the 7th fret of the fourth string with the third finger, then slide up to the 8th fret. While the 8th fret note is still ringing, use the first finger to play the 5th fret on the third string, so that the Bb and C notes resonate together.

For the next part of the phrase, barre your first finger across the top three strings at the 5th fret. Hammer onto the 7th fret of the third string with the third finger. Leave the third finger in place, then pick the second string, 5th fret (fretted by the barre) and hammer onto the 6th fret with the second finger.

That's a lot of explaining, but when you've done it once, you'll get the idea. You can also play the last two notes of the phrase on the first string without moving out of position if you like. The whole phrase should be played with a fluid, behind the beat feel.

Example 41

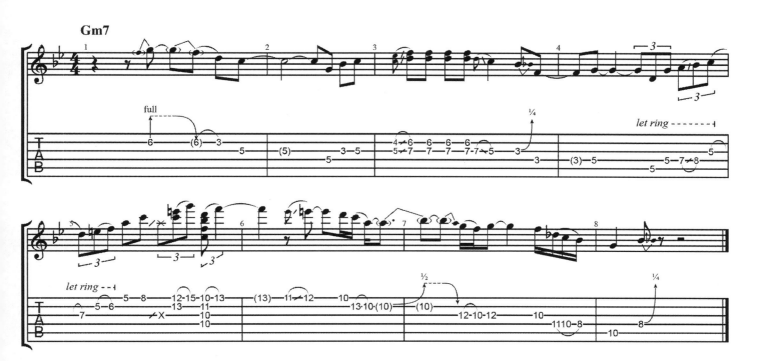

You should be able to identify the motif ideas that run throughout this final part of the solo, expressed in 6ths, double-stops and chord fragment ideas.

In bars 2-3, 6ths are always a useful way to spell out the harmony and are great for moving between positions and connecting ideas. Traditional blues-rock double-stops follow in bars 6-7. In bar eight, we're sliding back and forth using the top two notes of a Gm6 chord shape. In the final couple of bars, we bring everything back down to the G root note on the sixth string to end the solo.

Example 4m

I hope you have some fun piecing together the solo into a complete performance. As with every piece in the book, there is an audio track of the complete solo included in the download, so you can hear the whole thing performed as one piece. Then jam to the backing track and maybe pick just one of the ideas we've looked at (such as sidestepping) to focus on for a creative practice session.

Chapter Five – Minor Funk (Rhythm Part)

Over the next three chapters we're going to use a minor funk track as our workhorse tune and explore some different approaches to playing over it. It's reminiscent of the style of hard-hitting funk played by Tower of Power.

In chapters six and seven we'll get into some soloing concepts for this tune, but first let's look at its harmony and learn some rhythm guitar ideas that work over it.

In one sense, this whole tune is one big E minor vamp, pure and simple. When you listen to it, you'll hear that's all the bass guitar does – it just grooves away around an E minor tonal center. But to create interest and make the tune go somewhere, chords have been layered on top that work with the E minor bassline to enrich the harmony.

For example, you'll see that as the tune progresses, Gmaj7 and Gmaj7#11 chords are introduced. When a Gmaj7 chord (G B D F#) is played over an E bass note, the overall sound conveyed to the listener is that of an Em9 chord (E G B D F#). This "layered harmony" thinking runs throughout the tune and dictates the chordal ideas that are gradually introduced to take the piece in new directions.

Start by having a listen to the backing track and focus on what the bass guitar is playing. You'll hear that it's a syncopated part that contains a lot of fast staccato notes and rests. Underneath the bass, slightly back in the mix is an equally syncopated clav part. The challenge, when playing rhythm guitar on a tune like this, is to come up with a part that complements what the other instruments are doing and locks in with them, rather than getting in the way and making things too busy.

To open the tune, I wanted to play a funky single-note riff to create a kind of theme that I would return to later as a hook for the piece.

The hook is trickier to play than it looks on paper, but if you spent a good amount of time on the picking drills at the beginning of the book, you should be well prepared to tackle it. The key to playing this riff is to keep to strict alternate picking throughout, including for the muted accents, because most of the notes are grouped in fours.

On beat 3& of bar one, play a blues curl on the D note on the fifth string, 5th fret. The note is just pushed very slightly sharp. This little articulation somehow adds to the funk factor of the line.

Practice the first two bars to begin with and loop them around until you've nailed the lick. Bars 3-4 are similar, but other articulations are introduced in the form of slides. Work out a fingering that's comfortable to play the lick before you start.

Example 5a

After the four-bar introduction lick the first part of the tune kicks in, with the bass and clav driving the groove. At this point, the guitar part needs to become simpler and I favor a less-is-more approach. The idea here is to create a percussive groove from muted strums and pick out small, two-note chord fragments that pop out of the mix.

In jazz-funk music, the chords of the ii V cadence are often viewed as essentially the same sound. Let's imagine for a moment that the Em7 in our tune is a ii chord. It's accompanying V chord would be A7. If we ignore their root notes, Em7 and A7 make a very similar sound because they share important chord tones in common.

Here, you'll see that I play a fragment of an A7 chord, as well as stripped back Em7 voicings. This creates a Dorian sound over the E minor vamp, as if we are briefly playing in the key of D Major (Em7 is chord ii, and A7 is chord V in the key of D).

Example 5b

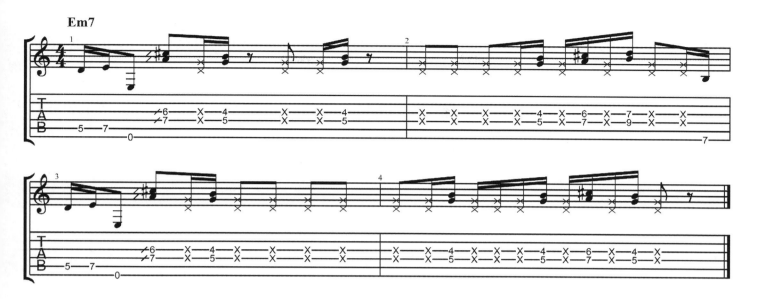

Example 5c takes the previous idea and varies it slightly for contrast. There are endless ways in which we could slightly change up this rhythm to create variations.

Example 5c

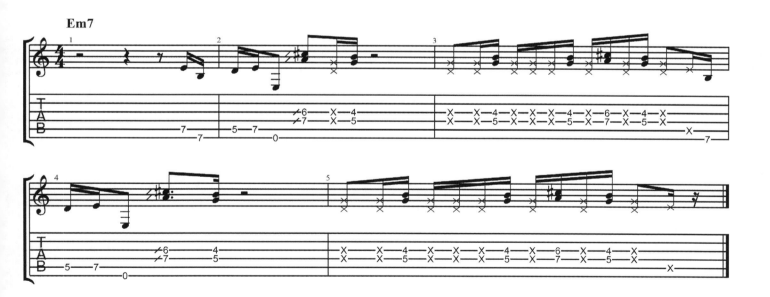

At this point in the tune, chords are introduced and there is a twelve-bar section that alternates between Gmaj7 and Gmaj7#11 chords. Because the keys of G Major and E Minor are relative, and because we're playing minimal, stripped-back voicings, a similar rhythmic idea will work just as well over these chords. All that's changed is the listener's perspective of the harmony.

Notice in bar four that the ascending chord voicings alternate between A7 and Em7. The C# note contained in the A7 voicing is also found in Gmaj7#11 (it's the #11), and the E note is the 13th.

Example 5d

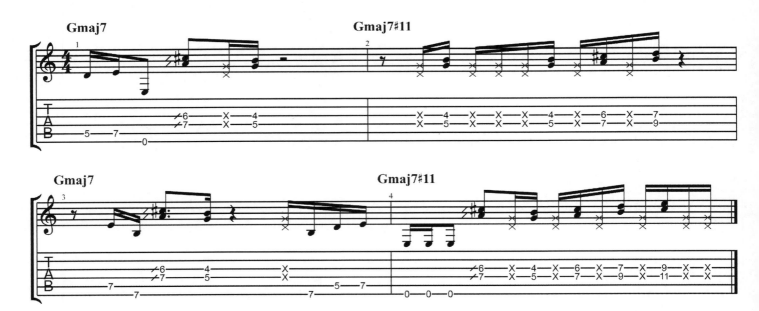

In the next part of the tune we come to a drum breakdown where no chords are played for four bars, before the introduction section kicks in again and we repeat the riff from Example 5a. Here it is again:

Example 5e

Now we're back into another E minor vamp section. Rather than repeat the idea we played in Example 5b, however, here's a more staccato variation on that idea with longer rests built in. Aim to get your timing as tight as possible here and really lock into the groove. Play with plenty of attack and punch this out. It could easily be a part played by the clav.

Example 5f

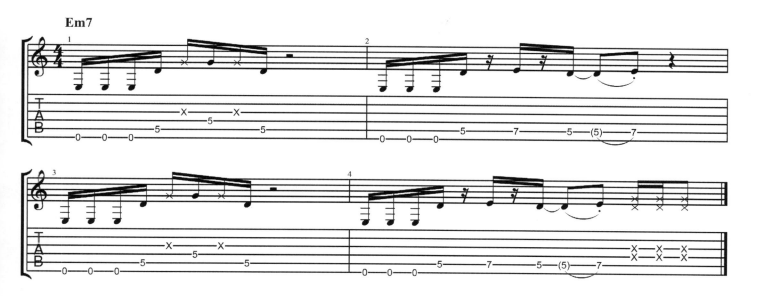

Now we move into the final section of the tune. It begins by repeating the G major 7 chord section, but then adds more chordal layers to open up the harmony.

This section can be divided into two, four-bar parts. In the first section we have:

| Gmaj7 | Gmaj7#11 | Am9 | Adim7 |

And the second section has a slight variation in bar four:

| Gmaj7 | Gmaj7#11 | Am9 | Adim7 Cdim7 |

The chordal layers add some rich tones to the harmony – especially the diminished voicings. We could analyze them in detail and consider the tension notes they create, but they are really just passing chords, designed to create a brief, cool sounding tension that quickly gets resolved. In the next four examples we'll look at some ideas to play over this section.

In bar one of Example 5g I begin by playing a D Major triad. Where does this idea come from and why does it work?

Remembering that the overall tonality of the tune is E Minor, playing D major over an Em7 chord creates a Dorian sound, an idea often used in jazz. We noted earlier that superimposing a Gmaj7 chord over an E bass note results in the sound of Em9, so the Dorian tonality fits well here.

Continuing this idea, bar two focuses on the A7 sound again, which over the Gmaj7#11 harmony creates a suspended sound that is resolved in bar three.

Bar four uses an idea that we'll discuss more fully in Chapter Seven when we discuss more advanced soloing. Briefly, we can add root notes to diminished 7 chords to "convert" them into dominant chords – which tend to be easier to deal with when we think about soloing. Adding a D bass note to an Adim7 creates a D7b9 chord, so here I'm playing fragments of a D chord over the diminished. More on this idea in due course!

Example 5g

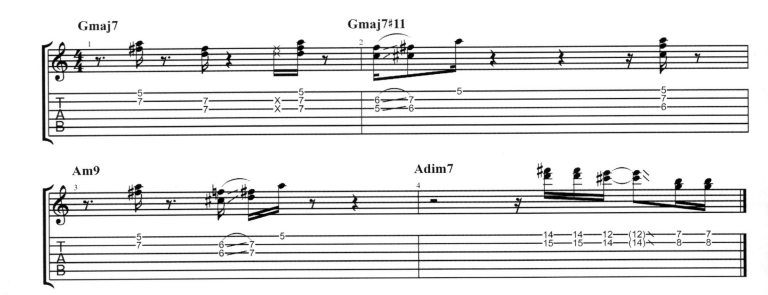

The next example includes some single-note fills for the first time in the rhythm part. It begins by highlighting the Gmaj7 chord and is based around this common Gmaj7 voicing:

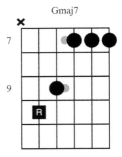

In bar three, the lick comes from the E Blues scale (E G A Bb B D) and is familiar blues vocabulary, but because we are superimposing it over an Am9 chord, it implies some colorful extended notes. The D note of the scale, for example, is the 11th of A minor, while the Bb note that is used throughout is the more colorful b9 tone.

Example 5h

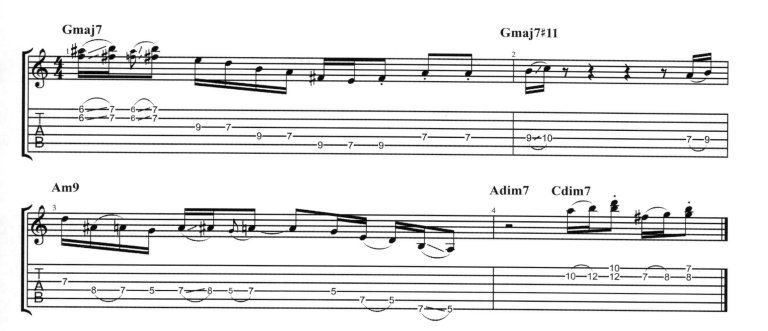

As this section of the tune turns around and begins again, we introduce some new ideas. Bars 1-2 of this example feature some bluesy double-stops that use notes from the G Major scale to highlight the harmony. The double-stop motif gets repeated in bar four.

Example 5i

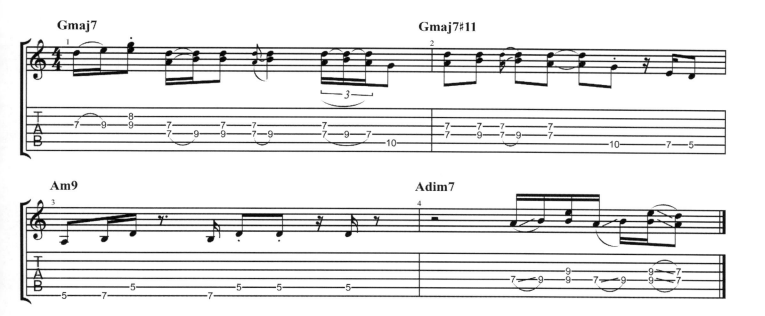

To close out the tune, one final new idea is introduced. Here the main thought was to use two-note structures voiced in 4th intervals to outline the harmony for a more angular sound. 4ths sound great when used over vamps and here we're using notes from the G Major scale to create the chord fragments.

In bar four, the first three notes are a fragment of a D7 chord, emphasizing the diminished-dominant chord connection we touched on earlier.

Example 5j

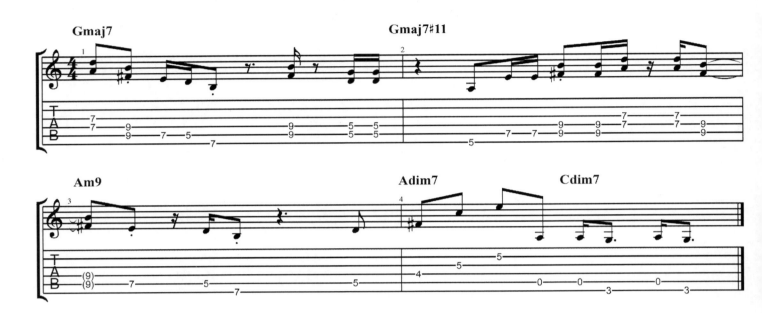

We've covered quite a few rhythmic and harmonic devices in this chapter, which can be used to create more interesting rhythm guitar parts. Groove and feel must always come first, but there's no reason why we can't add some sophistication too.

Spend some time jamming rhythm parts over the backing track for this chapter and see what ideas you can come up with. Try taking just one of the ideas we've discussed in this chapter and see if you can expand on it and create your own riffs.

Chapter Six – Minor Funk Soloing Approach

In the previous chapter we discussed the harmony of the minor funk tune we're working on, and looked at a range of approaches we can use to create appropriate rhythm guitar parts. Now we turn our attention to constructing soloing ideas over this piece.

Just like we did for the rhythm guitar, we're going to break down the tune into sections and learn some licks that work over each part. If you connect all the examples that follow, they form a complete solo for the whole tune.

In this chapter we're going to focus mostly on *motif building* and *articulation*.

If motifs are *what* we play, then articulation is *how* we play it. Note choices are important, but how we articulate a phrase has a huge impact on how it is communicated to the listener. Using different articulation techniques – such as bends, slides, legato, varying attack and volume, and playing unison notes – will help you to inject emotion into your solos and make them sing, rather than playing everything with a similar dynamic.

In this first example, the beginning of the solo is hinted at in the pickup bars, then a whole step bend targets the root of the Em7 chord in bar one.

Be sure to hit the bend on beat 1& of bar one, then release and re-bend the note a whole step. Release the bend once more, and this time slide from the 3rd to 5th fret to repeat the E note. I played this whole phrase off a single pick stroke on the first bend, then used its momentum to play the rest of the phrase with just the fretting hand. The result is that we hear the E note three times, but each time with a slightly different timbre and attack.

Notice that this phrase crosses the bar line. Phrasing across the line helps to create flowing ideas that don't sound like preconceived licks that fit neatly into each bar.

Listen to the audio and you'll hear the next phrase ends with a "lazy" bend. Deliberately bend this note up slowly, so that it cuts across the groove, and wring all the expression you can out of it. The bend targets an A note, which is a more colorful note to play over Em7 and not one of its basic chord tones. The A (11th) implies a cooler Em11 sound.

Example 6a

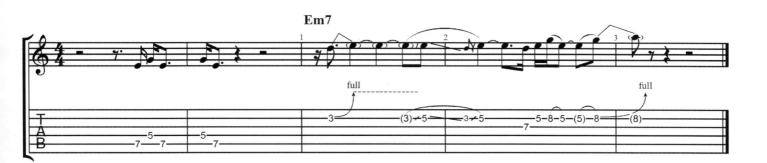

With an E minor based groove such as this, it would be easy to reach for E Minor Pentatonic ideas or the E Natural Minor scale. Of course, both scales would be perfectly good choices, but we can introduce some interest and tension by using alternative minor scales.

This is an idea we'll cover in more depth in the next chapter, but here I am alternating between the E Melodic Minor scale (E F# G A B C# D#) – mostly at the beginning of the lick – and the E Harmonic Minor scale (E F# G A B C D#) for the remainder of the line.

These two scales have just one note different – the C# of the melodic minor compared to the C of the harmonic minor – and I often view them as a single hybrid scale, or just a pool of notes to choose from.

After playing some low, rocky phrases with these scales, in bar four we begin an ascending motif idea, which will be developed in the next example.

Example 6b

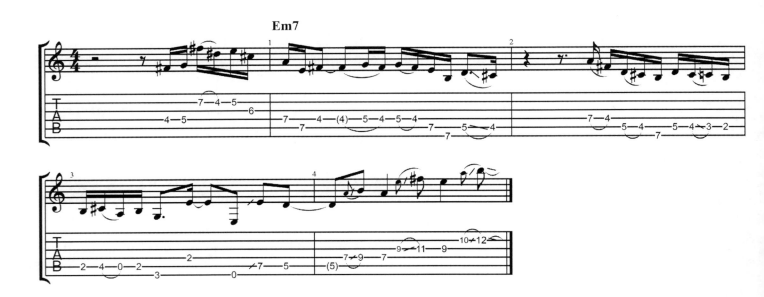

Bar one of this example dovetails with bar four of the previous one. The ascending run at the end of Example 2b leads to the simple motif idea of bars 1-2.

The first two notes of the motif highlight the 3rd (B) and 5th (D) of the Gmaj7 chord. The next two notes include the 3rd (B) again but add the more colorful 13th (E). Notice that the B note was relocated onto the third string to give it a different timbre.

The B note is repeated one more time, this time paired with the G root note of the chord. Check out the articulation on the audio to capture the feel – you'll hear that I pick the notes that follow each bend with a harder attack to make them sing out more.

The motif is followed in bar three with a fast descending run. This lick begins in 12th position – a location you'll be familiar with when reaching for the E Minor Pentatonic scale. If we add notes around that pentatonic shape, we have a useful shape for the E Natural Minor scale.

The diagram below shows the "box" shape for E Natural Minor in 12th position on the left. For this lick, I began with this shape, but then extended it downward, spreading the scale tones over a wider range of the fretboard, so that my shape looks more like the extended scale pattern on the right.

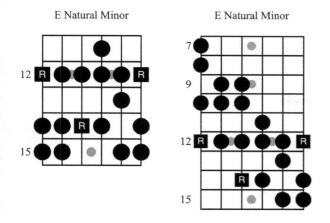

I omitted some of the natural minor scale tones and used pull-offs to execute the lick, legato style. The fast part is a series of 1/16th note triplets grouped in sixes. Plan how you're going to finger this lick beforehand and find a way that feels natural and comfortable to you. It's fine to play the line loosely over the beat – you don't need to be metronomic about it – this one's more about the feel.

Example 6c

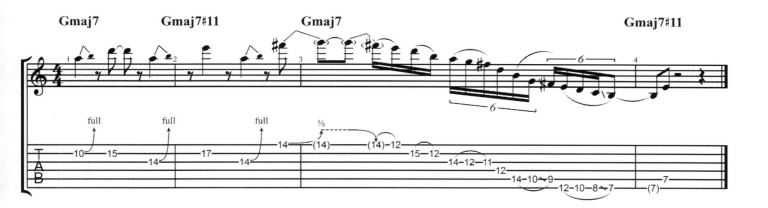

Example 6d states a simple motif and develops it through the middle two bars. Motifs can be note based or rhythmic. In other words, we can play unrelated notes but use repetitive phrasing to create a motif, as here. The pattern is a note played normally, followed by a bent note as we ascend.

The very last phrase of this line is a unison note lick. Here, the whole step bend on the second string, 15th fret, results in an E note, which is followed by an E played straight on the first string, 12th fret. Because the two E notes have a different timbre they create a kind of "out of phase" sound.

Example 6d

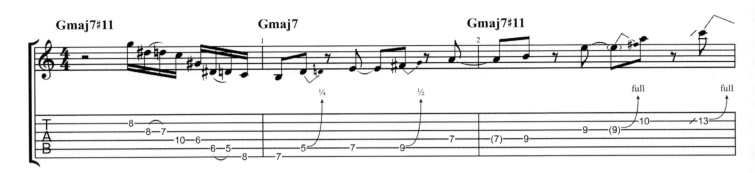

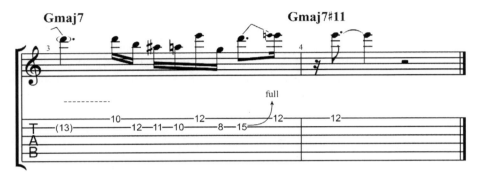

The next line begins with an opening lick in bar one before moving into a rhythmic motif for bars 2-3. The opening phrase uses the notes of the G Major scale and is based around the Gmaj7 shape below with its root note on the fifth string, 10th fret.

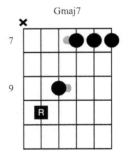

The first three notes include a high E note at the 12th fret, which can be reached with the fourth finger while the first finger remains anchored on the 7th fret. Although there is nothing special about the notes, the unexpected wide interval jump gives this lick a much more interesting shape.

You can see the shape that the motif takes from bar two by glancing at the TAB below. A double-stop on the top two strings is followed by a pull-off on the third string leading to one note on the fourth string. Execute each mini phrase with the following fingering:

Fret the double-stop with the first finger on the first string, and second finger on the second string. With those fingers still in place, hammer onto the third string with the third finger. Now, pull off with the third finger while jumping the first finger over onto the third string behind it. Follow this with the second finger on the fourth string.

It sounds complicated written down, but try it and you'll see that it's actually a very natural way to move the fingers. Once you've nailed the fingering it's the same for each phrase.

The second double-stop moves this shape down a whole step and the notes belong to the G Major scale. The two notes that follow it have also been transposed down a whole step, but the final note of the phrase only moves a half step (D# on the fourth string, 13th fret). This is a deliberate passing tension note, thrown into the mix to create some surprise. It resolves to the "correct" note (a D chord tone) when this phrase repeats as it crosses the bar line from bar two into three.

In bar three, the first double-stop combines A and F# notes. That combination implies a Gmaj9 sound over the harmony. As the shape moves down another whole step, root and 13th notes are paired.

When the double-stop shape moves down one final whole step, it's just about the repeating movement rather than precise note choices. Over Gmaj7, the F note produces a clash, as F# is the 7th of the chord, but our ears accept the dissonance because it's part of the rhythmic motif that has gotten us to this place in the music.

Example 6e

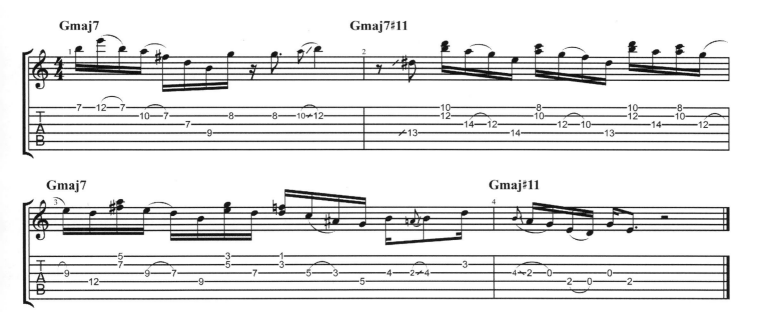

The next line takes place over the breakdown part of the tune, so there are no chords underneath to spell out the harmony. The lick is loosely based around the E Natural Minor scale, but it takes some twists and turns, deliberately stepping outside then back inside the harmony, using a sidestep.

The phrasing is tricky in bar two, so play this line slowly to work out the rhythm before attempting it at full speed. You can think of the phrase in the first half of the bar as five notes + four notes (three 1/16th note triplets and two straight 1/16th notes, followed by four straight 1/16th notes). The rhythm of this phrase is repeated for the second half of the bar. It's the change from 1/16th note triplets to straight 1/16ths that can trip you up, but persist and you'll nail it.

Example 6f

The next line brings us back into an E minor vamp section of the tune. We can take influence from any genre of music and in bar two of this example, the lick is a staple of country rock. The notes come from the G Major scale, but it's the type of idea that will work equally well over an E minor chord. This leads into a sliding double-stop in bar three that highlights the 5th and b7 of Em7.

The country rock vibe continues in bars 4-5. Here we are still thinking G major/E minor, scale-wise, and the line makes use of open strings. This part of the line is all about how we execute the articulation to inject as much feeling as possible into the phrases.

When playing the bend that begins at the end of bar three and spans into bar four, push it up slowly with a lazy feel. The B note we begin with is a chord tone of Em7, but the C# we're bending to is not (it's actually the 6th and creates an Em6 sound).

The group of notes that follow it are palm muted, plus we have to hop onto an adjacent string after playing the bend, so this calls for some deft fretting hand movement to make the transition seamless. The phrase carries over the bar line and finishes halfway through bar five. When playing the final slide from the 5th to 7th fret and back, just push the 5th fret note slightly sharp, like a blues curl. You'll hear it on the audio recording.

Finally, in bar six, when you hit the E note on the fifth string, 7th fret, apply some muting with the thumb behind the plectrum and pick the string hard to create a pinched harmonic.

Example 6g

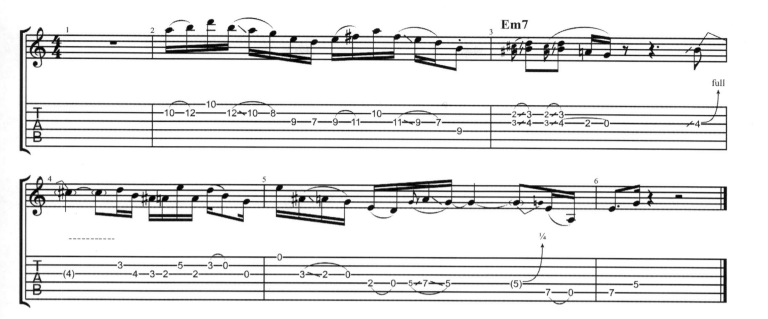

The next part of the tune is where the chord changes kick in and chord voicings are layered on top of the E minor groove to create different tonal colors. At this point in the piece, it felt right to state a simple melodic motif that sounded more like a melody than a lick. Over the next few examples you'll see that this motif is punctuated with other ideas, but we eventually return to it.

The motif includes a string skip and begins with B and F# notes (both Gmaj7 chord tones). In bar two, the phrase is adapted to fit the Gmaj7#11 chord. The F# note is bent up a half step to a G root note, and instead of returning to the B note of the previous bar, the phrase lands on a C#, which is the #11 tension note of the chord.

In bar three, the motif repeats, altered to fit the Am9 chord (using G and E chord tones), and the motif is resolved in bar four with a sliding note that targets the A root of Adim7.

Example 6h

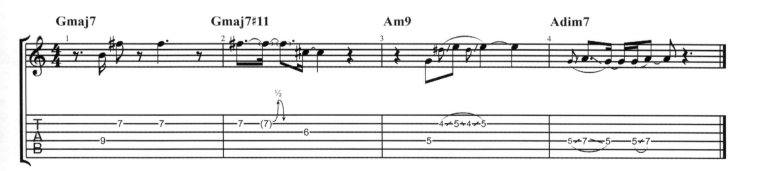

Following on from the motif, a new idea is stated in bar one of this example which takes a more intervallic approach. This opening phrase also has some palm muting applied.

The phrase in bar two uses the plain G Major scale for a hammer-on/pull-off lick with some string skips. Here I was visualizing the same 7th position Gmaj7 shape mentioned earlier, but this is another lick that would work equally well over an Em7 chord shape in the same location.

Listen to the audio and you'll hear that the line played in bar four sounds quite tense and "outside". We can always add tension to a solo by adding chromatic passing notes, i.e. notes that do not belong to the parent key.

One simple way of achieving those chromatic notes, often used by modern jazz-rock guitar players such as Oz Noy, is by using the sidestepping technique we discussed earlier.

The line in bar four is a *half step above* idea. In bar three I used notes from the E Natural Minor scale to form the melody, then visualized shifting that scale pattern up a half step to play around F Natural Minor in bar four. The result is a lick that contains several "outside" notes, but still has several E Natural Minor notes.

Example 6i

As the tune turns around for the final time, the motif stated earlier appears again briefly in adapted form in bar one. Once we've created a motif idea, we can use it as a kind of theme for the solo, much like a classical composer would, and return to it periodically.

Whenever the Gmaj7#11 chord comes up, a good scale choice for soloing over it is the G Lydian scale (G A B C# D E F#). G Lydian is the fourth mode of D Major, so it's like playing a D Major scale beginning and ending on the note G. This scale contains every note found in the Gmaj7#11 chord, so it fits perfectly.

In bar four, to spell out the sound of the Adim7 chord, we play another unison-style lick (this time repeating notes on the same string, rather than on adjacent strings). In each instance, the repeated note is an Adim7 chord tone.

Example 6j

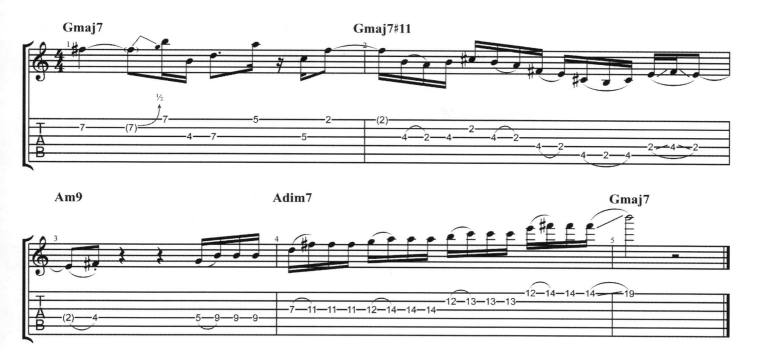

In order to force ourselves to be more creative with our lines, it's sometimes good to limit ourselves to one position or region on the neck, then work to get the most out of it. This self-imposed "limitation" often results in some great ideas, because it makes us think harder about both our note choices and phrasing. Here you can see that for most of bars 2-3, I limited the range of what I could play by remaining in 15th position, then gradually transitioning into 12th position. But I also limited my note choice by keeping the ideas on the top three strings for as long as possible.

This is an idea you can explore in your practice sessions. Put on a backing track then solo over it, limiting yourself to a small region of the fretboard, or to just a couple of strings. It's amazing how creative you can get even by limiting yourself to just one string!

Example 6k

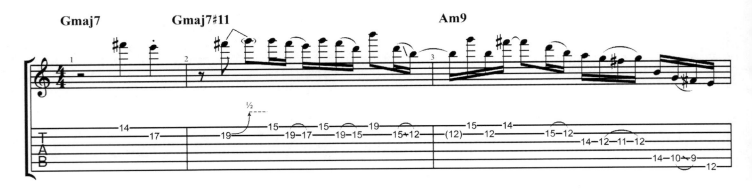

In the next chapter we'll explore some more advanced ideas over this tune.

Chapter Seven – Minor Funk – Advanced Soloing Ideas

In the previous chapter we worked through a complete solo for this tune, broke it down, and analyzed the ideas being used. Now we're going to learn another solo for the same tune, this time utilizing some ideas that push the boundaries of the harmony.

Here we're going to focus on two more of the soloing devices mentioned in the Introduction. This time we'll explore,

- The use of more colorful scales, to enable us to break away from the expected pentatonic vocabulary
- The use of chromatic passing notes to create "outside-inside" tensions (which work especially well over single chord vamps, but can be used with discretion over chord changes too)

Minor pentatonic vocabulary is a popular choice for soloing because it's easy to play on guitar and its harmony is so accessible. It's a very inside sound, so we need to look further afield if we want to create more excitement and harmonic richness.

This first lick gets straight into more colorful territory by using the E Melodic Minor scale in bar three to add some tension notes over the Em7 vamp.

Although this scale is used all the time in jazz, it could be seen as a more "exotic" scale choice for funk. However, it adds a cool combination of extended and altered tones to the harmony. The scale's F# note is the 9th of Em7, while its C# is the 6th. Then its D# note adds some chromatic passing note tension.

Example 7a

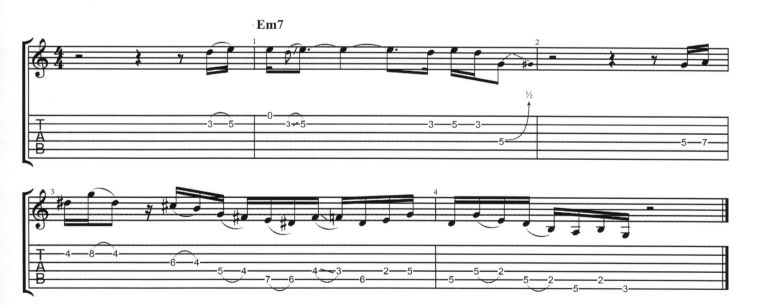

Creating a compelling solo is all about contrast. Contrast can be created using very simple phrasing devices (like playing low then high, playing slow then fast, or quiet then loud) or it can be achieved via our note selection e.g. sophisticated vs simple, or outside vs inside.

After the previous E Melodic Minor idea, this line is based around the E Blues scale, though it borrows an F# note from the E Natural Minor scale. The result is a bluesy hybrid scale, where the added F# note helps to imply an Em9 tonality.

Bar four uses mostly notes from the B Minor Pentatonic scale. Try using B Minor Pentatonic (but not the B Blues scale with its b5) over the Em7 chord.

Example 7b

The use of repetitive phrasing is a staple idea of the blues. This line mostly uses the augmented E Blues scale (E G A Bb B D plus F#) of the previous example. Because the F# is being played over a Gmaj7 chord rather than Em7, however, it implies the sound of Gmaj9.

Bar four uses the straight E Blues scale for the legato run. This lick makes use of open strings, so apply some picking hand muting if necessary to control the ringing. This phrase is played cleanly, rather than allowing the strings to resonate with each other.

Example 7c

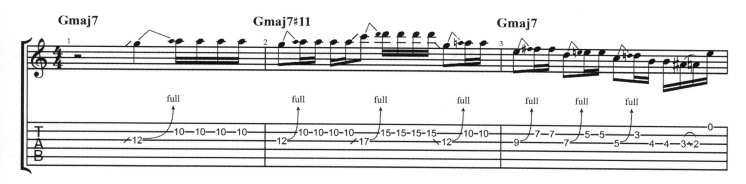

The line played over the next four bar section features some chromatic passing notes and uses the G Lydian scale mentioned in the previous chapter.

Peppering lead lines with chromatic notes can get messy and lack direction if we don't have a purpose for them, so I like to aim for a specific target. In bar two, I had two strong chord tones in mind – the 5th (D) and 3rd (B) of Gmaj7 – and the chromatic notes are being used to target them.

Bar three contains a sidestepping phrase that moves down a half step then resolves back up. From the end of bar two to midway through bar four, a descending motif moves inside and outside the tonal center. Sidestepping ideas are more about the movement of patterns than specific note choices, but they can yield some great results.

Example 7d

After the outside tensions of the previous idea, this lick brings some contrast with a motif development based around the E Blues scale. It grounds us firmly back in the overall E minor vamp harmony.

Example 7e

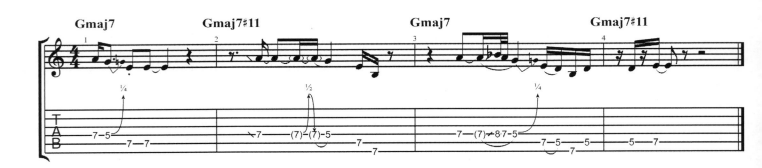

This example leads into the breakdown section of the tune. Since there are no chords here, the guitar can create some tension and basically go nuts! That is, as long as the melodic idea eventually resolves to the main tonal center.

After an opening blues-rock lick, bar three uses the G Lydian scale as its framework, with the addition of a couple of passing notes.

From bar four to partway through bar five, tension is added to the line with another sidestepping movement. The goal here is to resolve the lick to the E minor tonal center by the end of bar five. Bar four uses notes from the F Natural Minor scale, a sidestep movement a half step above, and by the end of bar five we've transitioned back into the E Natural Minor scale.

Example 7f

Bar one of this idea begins with an inverted Em7 triad to spell out the harmony. The beginning of the next triplet phrase adds in a D note (the b7), and the next phrase adds an A (11th) note to the mix of chord tones.

Bars 2-3 feature an E Minor Pentatonic scale phrase. In bar four, the G and D chord tones of Em7 are targeted from below using passing notes.

Example 7g

The next example begins by targeting the 7th chord tone (F#) of Gmaj7. When we encounter a chord like Gmaj7#11, we don't always have to scratch our heads and think, "What's the #11 note?" (it's C# by the way). The notes of a straight Gmaj7 will work, because Gmaj7#11 contains all of those notes too.

Whenever you see a chord on a chart that puzzles you, buy yourself some thinking time by focusing on the *basic chord tones*. You can think about adding those extended colors later.

Let me draw your attention to an idea I used in bar three.

When playing in a particular key, we can use arpeggios diatonic to that key and *superimpose* them over other chords belonging to the same key. We're in the key of G Major/E Minor here, but when we see a chord like Am9, we're not limited to playing an Am9 arpeggio over it. In fact, if we always spell out the changes that way, it can get a bit boring.

Instead, we can dip into the pool of other arpeggios that belong to the key center.

The harmonized G Major scale includes the arpeggios Gmaj7, Am7, Bm7, Cmaj7, D7, Em7 and F#m7b5.

Each of these arpeggios will have a slightly different effect when superimposed over another chord from the key.

In bar three, I chose to play an Em7 arpeggio pattern over Am9. In other words, chord vi in the key of G Major layered over chord ii.

What is the result of layering one arpeggio over the other?

Am9 comprises the notes A, C, E, G, B, while Em7 is constructed E, G, B, D.

Using an Em7 arpeggio here does away with the A root and also the C (b3). It highlights the 5th, b7 and 9th tones, and adds the 11th (D) to create a more sophisticated Am11 sound.

If I asked you to play an Em7 arpeggio, you'd do it very easily, but if I asked you to play an Am11 arpeggio that might require a bit more thought. Experiment with superimposing diatonic arpeggios and you'll discover some quick hacks to play ideas that include extended chord tones.

Example 7h

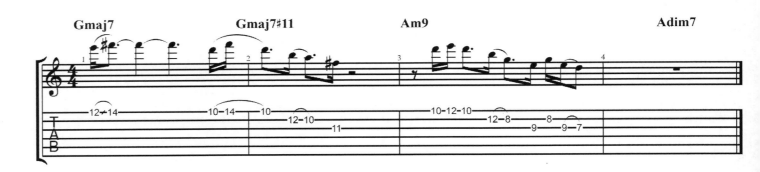

In the next line, the phrase in bar one uses the notes of the G Major scale and focuses on a rhythmic phrasing with dotted 1/8th notes to create a staccato feel that cuts against the underlying groove.

Bar two continues the G Major scalic idea. Notice the phrasing across this entire lick. In order to break away from predictable phrasing, the ideas begin slightly ahead of beat 1 of a bar, carry over the bar line, or leave a rest before they begin.

Not being controlled by the bar line is a great way to allow your phrases to flow. In bar two, the lick begins after a quick 1/16th note rest, and the last note of the bar carries into bar three, then resolves to a G note, the b7 of Am9. Similarly, in bar four, the phrase begins after an 1/8th note rest.

This is the section of the tune where the chord changes become more complex and, in bar four, we encounter the two diminished chords. I hinted at the *dominant-diminished connection* earlier. Now let's take a moment to look at this idea in more detail, so I can explain my thinking and approach to playing over these chords.

The first thing to note is that diminished 7 chords move across the guitar fretboard in minor 3rds (a distance of four frets including the first root note i.e. A to C).

Second, diminished chords are all inversions of themselves. Cdim7 contains the identical notes to Adim7, just in a different order. This means that whatever we decide to play over Adim7 will work over Cdim7 as well, and vice versa.

Third, if you add a root note to a diminished 7 chord, you create a dominant 7b9 chord, and as guitar players we naturally find dominant chords a bit easier to solo over than having to think about diminished scales.

To understand this idea, first play an Adim7 chord on the top four strings using this familiar shape:

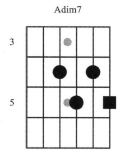

Now, reach your second finger across to fret a D bass note on the A string, 5th fret, and flatten your first finger slightly to fret the note previously held by the second finger. This forms a D7b9 chord.

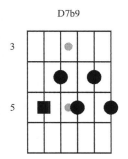

Jazz musicians call this relationship the *dominant-diminished connection*, where the addition of a new root note to a diminished 7 chord converts it to a dominant, and therefore opens up new tonal possibilities. It means that we can now base our solo lines around D7 whenever this bar of music occurs. Although it has taken a little theoretical explanation to get here, it's easy to think of adding that root note to form a 7b9 chord using the above shape.

The route I chose when soloing in this example was to view the D7b9 as a V chord. It could be the V chord in the key of G Major, or it could be the V chord in G Minor.

For a change of color and to add some tension, I opted for the latter, and the notes here originate from the G Harmonic Minor scale (G, A, Bb, C, D, Eb, F#), though I still added in a couple of passing approach notes.

Example 7i

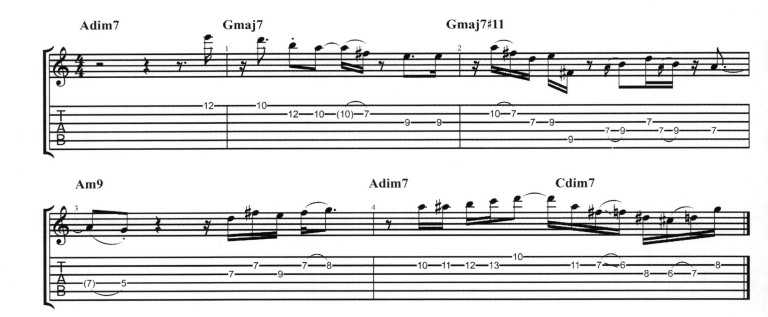

It's easier to construct melodic ideas if you can visualize chord shapes on the fretboard and work around them. In bars 1-2 of the next example, I'm visualizing two familiar Gmaj7 barre chord shapes, both with root notes on the fifth string, 10th fret.

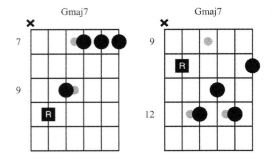

If you look at the note choices below you'll see that for the first half of bar one they are based around the first major 7 shape, then from halfway through bar one into bar two, we switch to the second shape, and all the notes are within easy reach of it.

In bar four, over the Adim7 chord, the notes are again from the G Harmonic Minor scale.

Example 7j

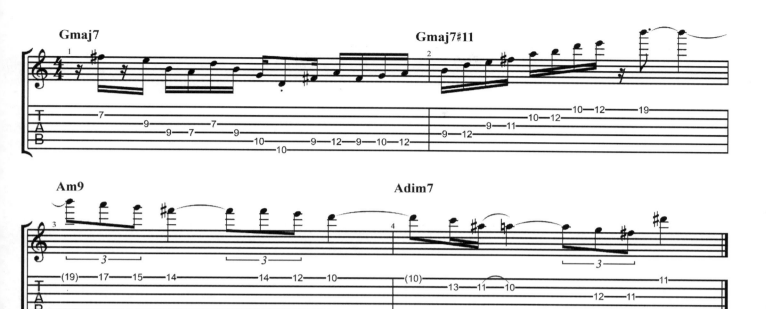

Here's a final idea over the closing section of the tune. This line is formed around the idea of repeating notes i.e. alternating between note choices to create a motif. It's often possible to say more with less – in other words, to limit the number of notes we play and get more out of them by way of rhythmic variety.

Over the Gmaj7#11 chord in bar two, for example, we limit ourselves to the root, 3rd and 7th chord tones and use a rhythmic phrase to highlight the chord.

In bar three, the lick uses notes of the G Major scale and, via repetition, emphasizes F# and D notes throughout. Played over an Am9 chord, these tones produce some colorful extended notes: F# is the 13th and D is the 11th.

Example 7k

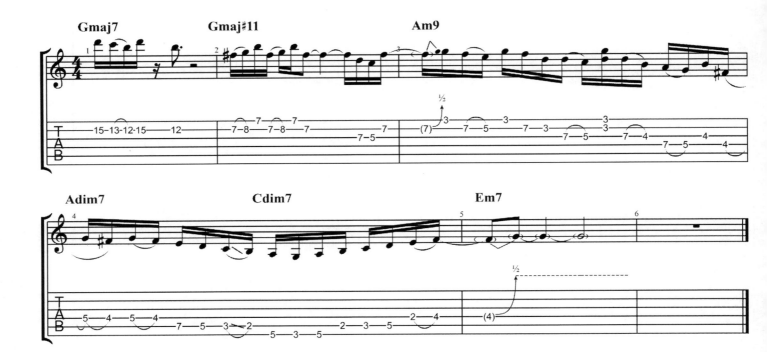

Now work on combining all the examples in this chapter to form another solo over the complete tune. Be sure to listen to the audio track of the full solo to guide you.

Conclusion

This has been a brief tour of the musical styles that were familiar to me, growing up in Louisiana, just outside of New Orleans. I hope you've had fun exploring this music and have learned some new ideas, or new ways of applying things, that will freshen up your playing.

At times, we've touched on concepts (such as arpeggio/scale substitution, or the minor six hybrid pentatonic scale) which in themselves could be huge areas of study for you. I recommend that you take just one idea that really appeals to you and work with it over *all* of the backing tracks, transposing it to different keys, until it becomes a part of your vocabulary. Then move onto the next idea and do the same.

Always keep listening to as wide a variety of music as you can, because as this book has hopefully shown you, there's something cool to learn from every style!

Have fun playing,

Shane.

Printed in Poland
by Amazon Fulfillment
Poland Sp. z o.o., Wrocław